A History of the Fly-by-Wire Jaguar

B.R.C. Weller BSc, CEng, MRAeS

FOREWORD BY DAVID M PARRY[1]

It is now a full forty years since Brian joined me in what was then the Jaguar project office to form the nucleus of the FLY BY WIRE implementation team. I greatly appreciate being invited to introduce Brian's history of the project, though it is perhaps difficult for someone with the direct involvement that I had to comment neutrally.

Following the formation of the British Aircraft Corporation in 1960, its constituent companies were substantially merged. By the mid-seventies the British aircraft industry faced imminent nationalisation and it was clear that nationalisation would quickly be followed by significant further mergers and rationalisation.

The management of the BAC Military Aircraft Division at Warton believed that the future of the Division would be determined by its competence in the key technologies that MoD/RAF requirements for the next combat aircraft would demand. Full time Fly-By-Wire was an essential one of these.

In the early seventies, I held the position of Chief Project Engineer on the Anglo-French Jaguar programme but by the mid-seventies the major part of development and production was complete and no major mid-life or other version updates were anticipated, so I was more than a little pleased to be offered a position in charge of a research programme I knew was seen to be as important as the Fly-By-Wire programme.

The structure of the technical team for the implementation phase was also adopted as something of a trial run for possible use on a full-scale Technology Demonstrator (the EAP).

The four years I spent on the programme were among the most interesting of the thirty-six years I spent with BAE Systems (or its predecessor companies). The work was even more satisfying as the programme led directly to my involvement in the EAP, P110, the 'Agile Combat Aircraft', the European Fighter and other Typhoon precursors as indeed it did for several of the team members.

Brian Weller has prepared a comprehensive and accurate account of the whole programme from concept to completion. In addition, he has clearly tried to give fair recognition to the many individual scientists, technicians, ground and aircrew who were involved, including many employed by our supplier companies (Marconi, Dowty and others) as well as RAE Farnborough. I believe he has achieved this. It certainly adds great interest, at least for those of us still alive! More important, in the long term, the work surely demonstrates, to all who may study it, the major contribution made by Jaguar Fly-By-Wire to the advancement of flight control into digital age aeronautics.

[1] David M Parry, FREng, FRAeS, BSc Eng (Hons), ACGI. Following the FBW Jaguar, he was Executive Director ACA until 1985 and then Director of all Warton Projects, and then all BAe Military projects after Warton merged with Kingston and Brough. He also acted as stand-in for Tony Baxter as General Manager Warton during 1988. Subsequently he was first Deputy Managing Director and then Managing Director of BAe Dynamics Group. He was appointed BAe Technical Director to the main board at the Strand in 1991. His final appointment was as Chief Executive at Royal Ordnance. He retired in 1997.

CONTENTS

List of Figures

List of Abbreviations

AC   Alternating Current
ACA   Agile Combat Aircraft
ACGI   Associateship of the City and Guilds of London Institute
ACT   Active Control Technology
A-D   Analogue to Digital
ADC   Air Data Computer
ADD   Air Stream Direction Detector
ADMC   Actuator Drive and Monitor Computer
ADR   Accident Data Recorder
AH   Ampère Hour
AICS   Air Intake Control System
AGARD   Advisory Group for Aerospace Research and Development
ATR   Air Transport Racking
BAC   British Aircraft Corporation
BAe   British Aerospace

BIT	Built in Test
CCV	Control Configured Vehicle
CRF	Continuous Recording Facility
CSAS	Command Stability Augmentation System
č	Manoeuvre Margin (percentage of wing mean aerodynamic chord)
D-A	Digital to Analogue
DASS	Data Acquisition and Simulation/Stimulation System
DBP	Dowty Boulton Paul
DC	Direct Current
DEC	Digital Equipment Corporation
DDU	Diagnostic Display Unit
DMA	Direct Memory Access
EAP	Experimental Aircraft Programme
EHP	Electro-Hydraulic Pump
EHSV	Electro-Hydraulic Servo Valves
EMC	Electro Magnetic Compatibility
EPROM	Erasable Programmable Read Only Memory
FIT	Failure Identification Table
FBW	Fly-by-Wire
FC	Flying Controls
FCC	Flight Control Computer
FCS	Flight Control System
FM	Frequency Modulation
FORTRAN	Formula Translation
FREng	Fellow of the Royal Academy of Engineering
FRG	Federal Republic of Germany
FRS	Flight Resident Software
GEC	General Electric Company [UK]
HF	High Frequency
HUD	Head Up Display
ITP	Intention to Proceed
LTU	Lateral Thrust Unit
LRMTS	Laser Rangefinder and Marked Target Seeker
LVDT	Linear Variable Differential Transformer

MAv	Marconi Elliott Avionics (later GEC Avionics)
MBB	Messerschmitt-Bölkow-Blohm
MDC	Miniature Detonating Cord
MDF	Master Data File
MoD	Ministry of Defence
MRCA	Multi-Role Combat Aircraft [early name for Tornado]
MS	Millisecond
NACA	National Advisory Committee for Aeronautics
NASA	National Aeronautics and Space Administration
PCM	Pulse Code Modulation
pDAS	programmable Data Acquisition System
PFC	Pre Flight Check
PCSP	Pilot's Control and Switch Panel
PFCU	Powered Flying Control Unit
PID	Proportional, Integral and Differential
PIO	Pilot Induced Oscillation
PROM	Programmable Read Only Memory
psi	Pounds per square inch
QPS	Quadruplex Position Sensors
RAE	Royal Aircraft Establishment
RAeS	Royal Aeronautical Society
RAF	Royal Air Force
RAM	Random Access Memory
RGU	Rate Gyro Unit
RSRE	Royal Signals and Radar Establishment
SBAC	Society of British Aerospace Companies
SDSP	Stall Departure and Spin Prevention
T/W	Thrust-to-Weight Ratio
TRU	Transformer Rectifier Unit
TSR.2	Tactical Strike Reconnaissance 2
TTU	Triplex Transducer Unit
U/C	Undercarriage
UK	United Kingdom
USA	United States of America
VHF	Very High Frequency

Acknowledgements

Illustrations are copyright of BAE Systems except as otherwise identified in the text.

Technical diagrams and figures have been re-drawn by the author from BAE Systems FBW Jaguar project originals, except Figure 2 which is based on 'C472/9, Concorde Engineering Notes, Section 9, Flying Controls and Flight Control System, 1973'.

In general the basis of this book is the author's memory of the project, together with reports which are now stored within the Heritage Department at BAE Systems at Warton. In respect of the flight test phase, it is based on the FBW Final Report, written by Terry Smith. Assistance was also received from Robin Heaps and Chris Bartlett (BAE Systems Rochester, retired), and John Steed (DBP, retired) as well as Phil Culbert, Andy Young and Dr Doug King who reviewed the text and made helpful suggestions for its improvement.

1   INTRODUCTION

This is the story of the Fly-by-Wire (FBW) Jaguar, an aircraft that is virtually unknown, even within the aircraft industry, but one without which the development of aircraft such as the Typhoon would have been impossible. In another respect, it could also be seen as an endpoint of the great flowering of innovation and research that took place during the fifties and sixties. Such research was not confined to any one country and led to great achievements such as Apollo and the Concorde. In fact, following the FBW Jaguar there has only been one other aircraft research programme in the UK / EU, namely the Experimental Aircraft Programme (EAP)[i].

The FBW Jaguar represented the final step in the development of aircraft flight control systems which saw the replacement of traditional mechanical flying controls by electronic links, so-called fly-by-wire. Fly-by-wire is now so common on both military and civil aircraft as to excite no comment; indeed, for the uninitiated, it seems the natural order of things given that digital systems and software completely dominate the world and are now poised to even drive cars automatically. However, not so long ago it was new and very much cutting edge, furthermore the difficulty of clearing the software for flight (safety critical software) was anticipated as being very difficult to achieve.

The aim of the Jaguar FBW research programme was defined as the design, development and demonstration of a safe, practical, full time, digital fly-by-wire flight control system for a combat aircraft. Throughout the programme, the flight control system was to be treated in all airworthiness aspects as though it were intended for production. Although it was not intended to demonstrate the aerodynamic benefits of active control technology (ACT), the programme did include flight demonstration of the aircraft in an unstable configuration in pitch and of a Stall Departure Spin Prevention System. Since the integrity standard of the flight control system was designed to be comparable with existing mechanical systems, and in addition, the aircraft was to be flown in an unstable configuration, it was decided early in the definition phase to remove all the mechanical control rods. Therefore, the FBW Jaguar quadruplex digital flight control system had no emergency back-up flight control system of any kind. This meant that on its maiden flight in October 1981, it was the first aircraft in the world to fly with a digital FCS without any form of back-up system.

This book describes the origins of the programme and its objectives, together with the approach taken to realise its aims. The selection of the aircraft in competition with Hawker Siddeley (Brough) was followed by the start of the main programme and aircraft conversion. The need for comprehensive testing meant that there was a need for extensive rigs, which were housed in a purpose-built extension to 7 Hangar at Warton. Later the Jaguar was flown to Boscombe Down for electromagnetic compatibility tests and it was one of the first aircraft to be subject to simulated lightning strike testing at Warton (with the assistance of the Culham Lightning Studies Unit).

Throughout the programme, the flight control system was treated in all airworthiness aspects as though it were intended for production; indeed, it could be said that 90% of the programme objectives were met when it was declared as safe to fly! In practice the flight trials demonstrated much more and included an assessment of an integral spin prevention system and aircraft configurations aerodynamically unstable in pitch.

Overall, the objectives of the programme were more than met in full, and its success is a lasting tribute to the combined efforts of British Aerospace[2], GEC Avionics[3] and Dowty Boulton Paul[4], together with the enthusiastic support of the MoD Procurement Executive and the Royal Aircraft Establishment.

1.1   Flight Control – In the Beginning

In September 1901 Wilbur Wright said[ii], 'When this one feature [meaning flight control] has been worked out, the age of flying machines will have arrived, for all other difficulties are of minor importance'. Without doubt, the Wright brothers were the first to fully appreciate that flying requires more than just a source of lift and forward propulsion – indeed they had cognisance of the whole problem of flight. Before they demonstrated powered flight they spent several summers at Kitty Hawk experimenting with gliders, discovering in the process that many of the then current assumptions about aerodynamics and flying were wrong. To investigate matters further, the Wrights built (in 1901) a wind tunnel to provide reliable aerodynamic data and lift coefficients for various wing shapes so as to achieve a better ratio of lift to drag, thus maximizing the range of their gliders and minimising the power needed from the engine for their momentous first powered flight in 1903.

What the Wright brothers understood was that an aeroplane operates in three dimensions; this may seem obvious today but did not to many of their contemporaries who saw aircraft control as analogous to that of a ship. On water, directional control is effected by means of a rudder and whilst aeroplanes do have rudders, they are not used for directional control. Only by the properly co-ordinated action of roll and pitch controls can the heading be smoothly changed; on the Wright Flyer this was done by wing warping (e.g. changing the camber of the wings) in roll and the use of a forward elevator for pitch. They also used the rudder to improve turn performance, initially linking it automatically to the warping controls and later giving the pilot the task of rudder co-ordination.

Although the Wright Flyer was a great achievement, it was not perfect, being somewhat unstable in pitch and requiring the constant attention of the pilot. It was also a very difficult aeroplane on which to learn to fly and there were many accidents. Consequently, there was plenty of incentive for other inventors and academics to better understand the underlying science and produce better machines. In Britain the focus of this work in the

---

[2] Now BAE Systems.
[3] GEC Avionics (or MAv), Flight Control Division at Rochester, is now part of BAE Systems.
[4] Dowty Boulton Paul is now part of Moog Controls.

run up to World War 1 was the Royal Aircraft Factory (later Royal Aircraft Establishment) at Farnborough. They designed the BE2, an aircraft which was sufficiently stable to be safely flown 'hands off' and hence ideal as a reconnaissance platform. The disadvantage of such high inherent stability was that it was not very manoeuvrable; losses were high when used above the Western Front against German fighters. Again, designers were spurred into action and manufacturers produced some much better aeroplanes specific to their intended role as fighters, such as the Sopwith Camel. However, the extent to which such aircraft were really 'nice to fly', judged by later standards, is another matter. The First World War was a tremendous stimulus to aircraft design in Europe, and to catch up the United States set up the National Advisory Committee for Aeronautics (NACA) to research into aerodynamics and related control problems.

By the 1920s, the task of aerodynamicists and control system designers (at that time they and the aircraft designers may have been one and the same) was becoming clear; aircraft were expected to be stable, controllable, and manoeuvrable and not to exceed the strength of the pilot![5] The emphasis on which of these requirements was most desirable depended on the role of the aircraft e.g. transport (stable) or fighter (manoeuvrability). The need for alleviation of the pilot's strength (or fatigue) was also becoming apparent with the increasing size and weight of aircraft and their increasing operating range.

Solving these problems took two main courses; alleviation of loads through mechanical/aerodynamic fixes e.g. trim tabs or servo tabs, and the development of the autopilot. The latter appeared surprisingly early with Lawrence Sperry demonstrating a gyro controlled stabilizer in 1914. The first commercial use of an autopilot took place in the early 1930s when Eastern Airlines fitted a Sperry A1 into a Curtis Condor (one of the last American biplane airliners). The capability of these really quite primitive autopilots was shown in dramatic fashion in 1933 when Wiley Post flew solo around the world, a trip that took from the 15th to the 22nd of July in a Lockheed Vega. By the mid-1930s, autopilots were under development or in production in many countries including the UK where Smiths produced a number of designs based on initial work by the RAE.

During the 1940s, the size and sophistication of aircraft increased considerably whilst the maximum range became essentially intercontinental. As a result, it became evident that manual controls, even with some assistance from servo tabs etc., would not be sufficient and a move was made to develop hydraulically powered flying controls. The De Havilland Comet, which first flew in 1949, was not only the first jet airliner, but also the first British commercial aircraft to have fully powered flying controls (whereas the later Boeing 707 reserved hydraulic assistance for the rudder alone).

As the 1950s dawned, military aircraft were pushing the transonic speed region or even going supersonic, again imposing new demands on their flight control system designers. Although powered controls solved some of the control problems associated with high-speed military aircraft, they were not a universal panacea and some 1950s aircraft were

[5] In Richard Smith's book, First Across, he mentions that during turbulent weather, the pilots of a Curtis flying boat (1919) had to work together to control the aircraft.

well known for their poor handling and susceptibility to spinning. To minimise drag they tended to be long and thin relative to the span of their wings, a characteristic that made them susceptible to the phenomena of inertial coupling, leading to loss of control.

Figure 1 US 'Century Series' in Flight (Clockwise from top F-100, F-101, F-102 and F-104 (NASA))

Of the above aircraft, perhaps the most notorious was the F-104, a Mach 2 fighter, which went into service with the German Air Force in the 1960s. Here the combination of difficult handling and poor training led at times to the loss of one aircraft a week.

These problems led designers in the late fifties and sixties to consider the use of electric signalling and analogue fly-by-wire systems whilst retaining mechanical controls for back-up in case of failure of the electrical or electronic elements. In Britain, advanced flying controls were seen as essential for two aircraft, Concorde and Tornado. In the case of Concorde, good handling was required over a speed range from low subsonic at take-off through to Mach 2. A further difficulty for a large supersonic aircraft is aerodynamic heating, which meant that Concorde's fuselage lengthened by almost a foot at full speed. The primary flight control system was provided by an electrically signalled system and duplex autopilot, but the need to retain mechanical back-up resulted in considerable system complexity and weight; however, at the time there was not sufficient confidence in electrical signalling to eliminate mechanical reversion. A simplified view of only part of the Concorde FCS [iii] illustrates the problem of hybrid electro-mechanical systems.

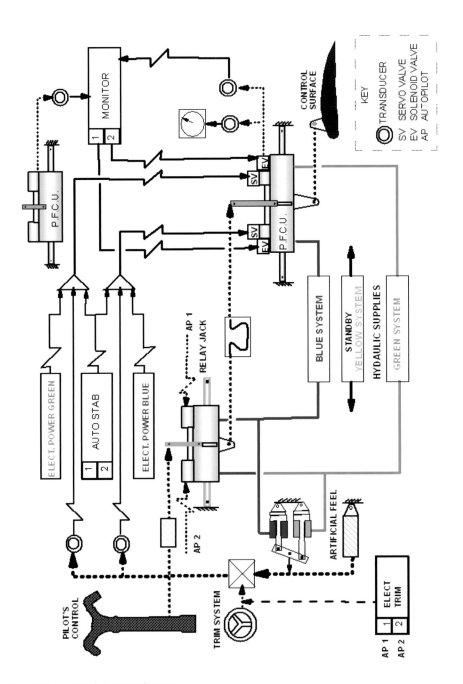

Figure 2 Concorde's Flight Control System

Tornado's FCS has a primary electrical Command Stability Augmentation System (CSAS) with mechanical back-up. The CSAS consists of a triplex analogue fly-by-wire system feeding into electro-hydraulic actuators. Separate pitch and lateral computers, rate gyros and pick-ups for the pilot's controls are provided. There is also a direct mechanical link to the taileron actuators for reversionary control in the event of failure of the electrical system[6]. No direct link is available to the rudder, which is centred after electrical failure. Further 'black-boxes' provide for the autopilot (duplex digital) and for the Spin Prevention Incidence Limiting System (SPILS), a late addition. Additional complexity is introduced by the wing sweep system and its associated links to the leading edge slats. Overall system complexity, in terms of the number of black boxes, actuators and mechanical rods is considerable[7]. Consequently, the system is both heavy and demands a good deal of maintenance. However, at the time the aircraft was designed, this was the only approach possible to achieve the performance desired, and in this objective its designers were entirely successful.

1.2   Full Time Fly-by-Wire

The route to full time fly-by-wire (FBW), without mechanical backup, was via rockets and the Apollo programme. With missiles there was no background of manual control and so the natural way to control such vehicles was by automatic systems carried on-board the rocket. The origin of this development was the wartime effort directed by Werner von Braun at Peenemünde. The A4 (or V2) rocket depended on quite a sophisticated control system of gyros, amplifiers, servos etc. to stabilise what was essentially an inherently unstable vehicle[iv]. Amazingly, both 'strap down' and 'inertial platform' arrangements were developed with preference being given to the simpler and cheaper 'strap down' arrangements. From today's perspective, it was clearly the precursor of the various American missile and rocket programmes of the fifties and sixties. Indeed von Braun and his team were relocated to the US Army's Redstone Arsenal where they designed the Redstone and Jupiter 'C' missiles. With the transfer of the Redstone Arsenal to NASA in 1959, the same team was then responsible for the Saturn programme.

A generic FBW system consists in essence of three main elements:

• An inertial measurement device (as a minimum, rate gyros)

• An amplifier to sum command with feedback

• Some form of servo or power control actuator

---

[6]Interestingly enough, using the 'numbers game' the CSAS is inherently just about reliable enough to be used without any form of back-up, but the complexity introduced by the back-up system, makes its presence essential.

[7]A further difficulty introduced by a mechanical back-up is that the system as a whole is more susceptible to defects caused by foreign objects becoming jammed in the control system. On the 28th of September 1996, Tornado ZE759 was lost off Blackpool because a loose bolt became jammed in a taileron actuator. Happily, the pilot and navigator (Paul Hopkins and Al Reynolds) were able to eject safely.

In addition, if fully automatic control is required (as is obviously essential for a rocket or guided missile), then some form of memory (to store the desired course) becomes essential.

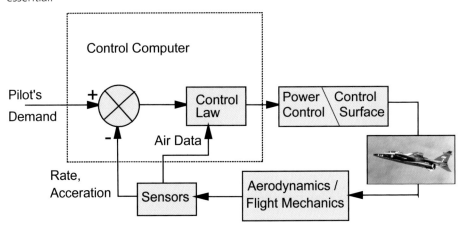

Figure 3 Basic fly-by-wire Flight Control System

The diagram shows, in simplified form, one axis of control. The benefits of FBW are considerable and were both understood and quantified before any such aircraft had flown. They may be summarised as follows:

- Improved handling qualities optimised across the flight envelope, e.g. manoeuvre demand
- Mechanical friction and backlash can be minimised
- Undesirable trim changes are eliminated
- 'Carefree handling' through automatic protection against stall, departure and over-stressing of the airframe (g-limiting)
- Reduced maintenance costs, resulting from the reduction in mechanical complexity
- Makes possible the 'controlled configured vehicle' (CCV) (i.e. an aircraft wholly dependent on its FCS for stability) hence:
    - Weight reduction
    - Improved aerodynamic efficiency
    - Improved performance e.g. better manoeuvrability

The last point is frequently described as the advantage of the aerodynamically unstable aeroplane. To understand why this should be the case it is necessary to look more closely at what is meant by 'stable' versus 'unstable' aircraft. In a conventional stable aircraft it is generally arranged that the centre of gravity is ahead of the centre of lift and thus has to be balanced by a download on the tailplane, as is illustrated in the following figure.

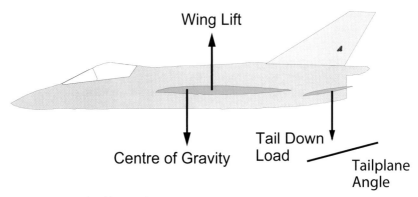

Figure 4 A Conventional Stable Aircraft

Clearly, in this case the wing has to be big enough to support not only the weight of the aircraft but also the down force on the tail. This configuration is said to be stable because any disturbance tends to die out naturally. For example, if the angle of incidence increases (the aircraft is inclining upward) then the lift from the wing increases and the download from the tail is reduced. This gives rise to a couple, acting anti-clockwise in the above example, thus tipping the nose down and restoring equilibrium.

For an unstable aircraft, things are rearranged as shown below:

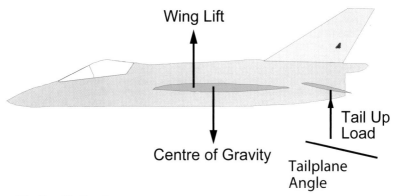

Figure 5 The Unstable Aircraft

Here the tailplane contributes to lift, enabling a smaller wing to be used for the same net lift. The disadvantage of this arrangement is that it is inherently unstable in the absence of an active control system. Taking the same case as before, a disturbance tipping the nose up leads to an increase in wing lift, which, being ahead of the centre of gravity creates a couple giving rise to a further increase in incidence. This process happens very rapidly; the term used is time to double amplitude and in the case of the Jaguar when configured for maximum instability, this was only 385ms.

The extent of improvement possible by use of the controlled configured vehicle concept was set out by B.R.A. Burns (then deputy Head of Aerodynamics) in his 1978 paper[v]. By optimising the design of aircraft to take advantage of an active control system, very useful improvements can be made which can be summarised by comparing the mass of aircraft for the same role (payload and radius of action). Typically, for the same task, an aircraft that is aerodynamically unstable (and thus reliant on its control system) will be 9% lighter, and similarly have 9% less drag. This translates into a smaller (and hence cheaper) aircraft with a smaller engine, the latter resulting in lower fuel and operating costs.

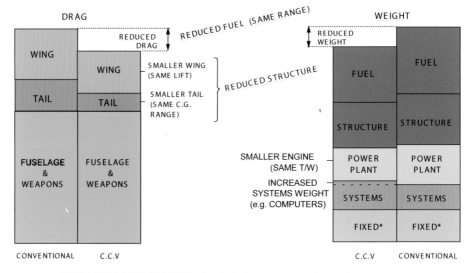

* FIXED WEIGHT INCLUDES WEAPON LOAD, CREW AND SUPPORT SYSTEMS
‡ NOTE THAT THE STRUCTURE WEIGHT IS ALSO REDUCED BY THE ABSENCE OF BRACKETS AND OTHER SUPPORTS FOR CONVENTIONAL CONTROL RODS.

Figure 6 CCV and Conventional Aircraft – A Comparison

The 'Systems' box on the diagram may need some comment, as it is frequently ambiguous as to whether FBW aircraft have heavier or lighter systems. Clearly a FBW aircraft has equipment not possessed by conventional ones, e.g. flight control computers, rates sensors etc. However, it also avoids many parts necessary in ordinary mechanically signalled systems, such as control rods, complex feel systems and other parts (such as autopilot computers), which may be an inherent part of a FBW system. Undoubtedly, the worst position for complexity and weight is the hybrid half-way-house, where a basically FBW aircraft also has a mechanical back-up system. Alternatively, an essentially mechanical FCS may require a high authority autopilot for some flight critical modes such as terrain following (e.g. F-111). Such hybrid systems were fairly common in the early days of military FBW (e.g. Tornado) and as a result their flight control systems tended to be significantly more complex and heavier than their successors.

For example, the weight of an actuator combining both mechanical and electrical inputs might be twice that of a pure FBW device. Combined actuators (i.e. FBW plus mechanical back-up), may well also possess many more high precision parts (perhaps by a factor of ten), which are subject to wear and therefore require periodic maintenance. Overall, although the systems weight for the Jaguar went up, this was on an aircraft that was not originally designed for FBW and hence not optimum in terms of equipment installation.

Early FBW systems used analogue technology, but world aircraft manufacturing companies began serious studies into digital control systems, fly-by-wire and Active Control Technology (ACT) in the early 1970's. The British Aircraft Corporation (BAC) (which later became part of British Aerospace and hence BAE Systems) was no exception. A study was made as early as 1972 to assess the effect of artificial stability on the design of a low altitude strike aircraft, taking the Jaguar as a datum. Soon after studies began, the benefits of electrical signalling and electronic feedback control to provide artificial stability became readily apparent. In 1973, BAC made a joint proposal with Messerschmitt-Bölkow-Blohm (MBB) for a CCV research program (pitch axis only) based on a Jaguar test vehicle. However, this proposal was not accepted and MBB later proceeded with their own programme[vi] based on an F-104 aircraft.

By the mid 1970s, there was considerable momentum towards full time FBW. In the United States, this led to the development of the well-known and highly successful F-16, initially with an analogue flight control system. Meanwhile, in the UK a full scale research programme was about to be launched with the aim of designing and testing a digital FBW aircraft which from the start would fly without any form of backup i.e. it would have no reversionary analogue or mechanical system. At the time, this was a bold step as the only real precursor was the NASA F-8 digital FBW demonstrator (first flight May 25, 1972). That aircraft used a single Apollo Lunar Guidance Computer together with a triplex analogue backup system; hence, failure of the digital computer or its software was not necessarily safety critical. Consequently NASA avoided, to some extent, the need to fully qualify digital hardware and software. What the F-8 did do was to demonstrate that it was perfectly feasible to control an aircraft using a digital computer: albeit that problems were encountered in respect of pilot induced oscillation owing to the low update rate of the lunar guidance computer and other system lags. Another point noted was that a large team of system and software engineers/programmers was available to NASA as a follow on to Apollo; to be practical (i.e. cost effective) on an ordinary aircraft the design and clearance process would have to be considerably streamlined and simplified.

Figure 7 The NASA F-8 Research Aircraft (NASA)

1.3   Feasibility Study

BAC issued a research paper[vii] in July 1974 proposing the use of a Jaguar as the test aircraft in partnership with Smiths Industries as electronic supplier. Shortly thereafter, a contract was received from the MoD to carry out a feasibility study in line with that proposal and work began in earnest in November 1974. These studies included system safety requirements and the impact they were likely to impose on system design. Initially the contract did not cover any involvement by an actuator supplier, but as early as the first progress meeting (December 1974) BAC requested that this should be remedied. Some discussions had already taken place with possible actuator suppliers and as a result, Dowty Boulton Paul (DPB) was recommended as the most appropriate partner.

During 1974, Hawker Siddeley Aviation Ltd. (Brough) also carried out preliminary studies into the benefits of FBW and issued study papers recommending detailed research into advanced control systems. The emphasis of their work was into the benefits of FBW, such as manoeuvre demand systems, direct lift or side force control and was, in the range of aerodynamic topics covered, probably of great interest and attractive to the RAE. In comparison with BAC, there was little mention of airworthiness matters or the problems associated with the use of digital computing for flight[viii] control[ix] .

At Warton, B.R.A. Burns (Sandy Burns) led the feasibility study and involved engineers from several departments and sites in order to gain from as much existing expertise as possible. The author joined the team from Filton having previously worked on Concorde's Air Intake Control System (AICS). The AICS was the first civil safety involved digital control system, and was critical to aircraft performance; it was the excellent air intake design on Concorde that allowed the aircraft to cruise supersonically without re-heat, unlike the

Russian Tupolev Tu-144 'Concordski'. Other members of the team included Brian Gee, John Gibson, Ian Darbyshire, Mike Walker and Ken Carr (aerodynamics), Gordon Lewis and John Holding (hydraulics and actuation) Dave Musson (airworthiness) and Dave Whittle (systems).

Once the team was identified, work progressed rapidly during 1975 and meetings were held with the various stakeholders. Several of these meetings took place at Smiths' facility at Cheltenham. This was quite popular with all concerned because of the rather good lunches provided. In addition, the approach of Smiths tended to be quite academic which suited the monitors from RAE Farnborough. Dr Meredith was their chief theorist and produced several papers dealing with the possibility of various obscure data transmission problems that he called the Echo and Iago effects[x].

One side effect of the Smiths' lunches was to make the participants somewhat drowsy. This gave Sandy Burns the opportunity to demonstrate a quite amazing ability – he managed to take the meeting minutes even though he appeared to be asleep (but in reality clearly was not!) For participants from Warton, returning north along the M5, sleep was the best answer after an early start and demanding meetings, provided one was lucky enough not to be driving. Looking back with the benefit of hindsight, this part of the programme was very worthwhile and a great deal was learnt through discussions with Smiths.

The Feasibility Study lasted until September 1975 and a report was issued[xi] summarising the results in some detail. It was concluded that it was essential that the design of any new aircraft relying on FBW must be preceded by a demonstrator programme. This would allow a satisfactory flight control system to be designed and the inevitable development problems identified and solved. Further, such a programme would also permit appropriate production design criteria, including airworthiness requirements, to be specified for the next aircraft.

The primary objective of such a programme was therefore stated as being:

• To generate confidence in the airworthiness of full time fly-by-wire

This proposition was accepted by the MoD, which subsequently issued a request for proposal in 1976. Both BAC and Hawker Siddeley (Brough) responded and submitted proposals. BAC naturally used the Jaguar, whilst Hawker Siddeley's proposal was based on the use of a Buccaneer. Following evaluation of the proposals, MoD, and their technical advisers at the RAE, selected the BAC / Jaguar bid rather than that from Hawker Siddeley.

The difficulties of embarking on such a programme were considerable, not just from a purely technical aspect but above all because whatever was produced had to be capable of being certified as safe to fly. The route to full certification was initially unknown and had to be devised if the programme were to progress. This inevitably meant that the working procedures also had to receive attention at the start of the programme, and to paraphrase Donald Rumsfeld, there were many known unknowns and as it turned out a good many unknown unknowns.

Fortunately, there were two UK programmes to draw on directly for information and guidance. Firstly Concorde, which as well as its electrically signalled FCS also had a full authority digital Air Intake Control System (AICS). The AICS was another world first as the earliest application of digital control to a critical civil airliner system. The second programme was the Tornado (then known as the Multi Role Combat Aircraft or MRCA) with its triplex analogue FBW system and mechanical backup. Since engineers from both these programmes joined the FBW Jaguar team, it was able to directly benefit from this experience. From the Concorde AICS came general digital system knowledge and some understanding of methods applicable to the system analysis and clearance. Tornado's main influence was felt in two areas; that of control law design, and secondly a determination to avoid the complexities of mixed mechanical/electrical hydraulic actuators (i.e. to avoid a FBW system with mechanical back-up or hydro-mechanical voters).

Some limited experience was also available from the Royal Aircraft Establishment (RAE) Farnborough, which carried out two programmes that are not particularly well known, during the sixties and seventies. The first involved the modification of the AVRO 707C to carry out research into handling qualities and inceptor design (i.e. the pilot's controls). Specifically, it investigated rate demand systems, and made a comparison of the qualities of side stick versus 'conventional' centre sticks. The programme concluded[xii] that the solution for the future would be an electric signalling system with no mechanical back-up; reversion to a 'get you home' mechanical system was seen as adding a great deal of extra mechanical complexity and is problematic for the pilot by virtue of the need to train for what may feel like two different aeroplanes. It was also concluded that there was a strong preference for a centre stick rather than side (the latter being chosen by General Dynamics for the F-16).

Figure 8 The Avro 707C (in Cosford Museum (author))

The second RAE programme converted a two-seat Hawker Hunter to fly-by-wire using a quadruplex analogue FBW system, but retained mechanical back-up. This programme was unfortunately cut short because of a severe engine failure and fire, which fortunately took place on the ground allowing the pilot to escape, albeit with some injuries.

BAC's Feasibility Study had included a survey of all known FBW programmes (to mid 1975). A summary of the results was produced and is reproduced below:

Aircraft Type	Country	Status	System	No. of axes	Back-up	Flight Date
Avro 707[8]	UK	Research	Analogue	2	Mech.	1953 (Original aircraft)
F-8	USA	Research	Simplex Digital[9]	3	Triplex Analogue	1972
F-4	USA	Research	Quad. Analogue	3	None	1972
Hunter	UK	Research	Quad. Analogue	3	Mech.	1974
MRCA (Tornado)	UK	Production	Triplex Analogue	3	Mech. (Tailerons only)	1974
YF-16	USA	Development	Quad. Analogue	3	None	1974
Sea King	UK	Research	Triplex Analogue	N/A	Mech.	1976
F-104	FRG (West Germany)	Research	Quad. Digital	3	Mech.	1976
F-16	USA	Production	Quad. Analogue	3	None	1977
Jaguar (Proposed)	UK	Research	Quad. Digital	3	None	1980 (Planned) (Achieved 1981)

Programmes reviewed during the Feasibility Study with actual or projected flight dates

[8] The Avro 707C programme is included here for completeness, but was not formally reviewed as part of the Feasibility Study.
[9] The F-8 used an Apollo Lunar Guidance Computer and Inertial Measurement Unit.

1.4   The Main Programme

Company activity started in earnest following selection and the MoD's intention to proceed (ITP), although the full contract was not received from the MoD until mid 1977. Equipment, particularly the Flight Control Computers (FCCs) and primary actuators, was subject to competitive tendering following the ITP.

In respect of the FCCs, bids were received from Smiths (the feasibility study partners) and Marconi Elliott Avionics (MAv). Following evaluation of both the technical and commercial proposals, Marconi Elliott Avionics at Rochester Kent was selected to provide the electronics, based on significantly lower costs (£1.5M versus £3M) and by their offering a fixed price bid whereas Smiths' was cost plus. The decision by Marconi Elliott to offer a low cost bid to trump Smiths clearly reflected their determination to dominate the new FBW equipment market in the following decades. In spite of their considerable experience, the programme turned out to be something of a baptism of fire and a very steep learning curve for those concerned. The actual cost turned out to be about twice their 'estimate' and the overrun had to be largely borne by MAv. Problems arose from an underestimate of the size of the software task, under-skilled software sub-contractors and a lack of configuration control. This placed a lot of strain on the original management team. Overall, from a MAv company perspective, it was a very successful strategy as it led to significant contracts for FBW systems for both military and civil aircraft (e.g. Typhoon and the Boeing 777).

The possible actuator suppliers included Lucas, Fairey (who already supplied FBW actuators for Tornado) and Dowty Boulton Paul (DBP). DBP was selected to supply the actuators. Here there was less effective competition because it was the DBP actuator concept (duo-triplex and failure absorbing) that effectively determined the layout of the rest of the system. That said, Fairey's had also proposed something similar to Smiths during the feasibility study[xiii]. However, Fairey was at that time busy with the Tornado actuators whilst DBP were looking for something new and advanced to follow on from their actuators for Concorde. As with MAv, the FBW Jaguar work placed DPB in a very favourable position for future work since they went on to provide actuators for the EAP and Typhoon.

The original intention was to fly in 1980, but a combination of technical difficulties and late equipment delivery (especially software) delayed matters until 1981. The final programme achieved is shown below.

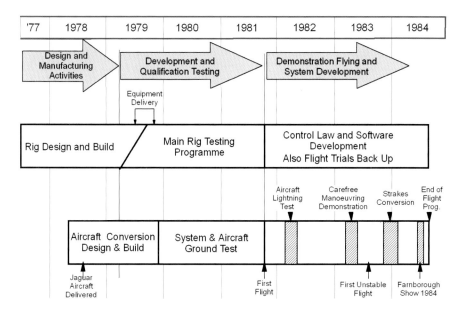

Figure 9 Programme Timescale

1.4.1   Experience – Suppliers

Marconi-Elliott's experience was considerable in terms of analogue autopilots (e.g. for Concorde) together with the analogue Command Stability Augmentation System (CSAS) for Tornado. Digital work included the Tornado autopilot (duplex) and the much more significant Electrical Flight Control System for Boeing's YC-14 short take-off demonstrator aircraft. The latter system consisted of a high authority triplex (fail-operational / fail-safe) set of electronics. Initially they proposed the use of the processor designed for the YC-14, but this was found to be inadequate for the Jaguar. A more powerful one was designed for the Jaguar using the same instruction set, so that their YC-14 software could have been re-used had that aircraft gone ahead into production.

Dowty Boulton Paul had designed the actuators for Concorde and this formed a very useful bank of knowledge and the basis of a prototype 'breadboard' actuator together with rigs and test equipment. They also were responsible for the actuators for the RAE's Hunter FBW demonstrator, and subsequently those for EAP and Typhoon.

1.4.2   Experience – BAC / BAe

In terms of experience, BAC was in the fortunate position of having two programmes providing relevant knowledge. Firstly, there was Tornado with its triplex CSAS and digital duplex autopilot; however, primary responsibility for the design of the Tornado flight control system resided with MBB (located in Ottobrunn, near Munich). Fortunately, there was at Warton an aerodynamics development team, the main hydraulics rig and flight backup rig. In addition, the Production and Development Test department (known to all as P&D Test) was also developing its skill base through the support of Tornado. The second source of expertise came from Bristol. Although it might have been expected that this would have been from the Concorde flight controls group it was in fact from the Guided Weapons Electronics and Space Systems Division. This was because that department had been given responsibility for Concorde's duplex digital Air Intake Control System; the world's first safety involved digital system on a commercial aircraft.

It was also possible to study published papers released by NASA, but in those pre-internet days, access was not the simple matter it is today. The two principal sources were an AGARD published book about the Apollo guidance system[xiv] and a paper about the F-8 FBW demonstrator [xv].

In theory, information should have been available from RAE Farnborough (the programme monitors on behalf of the MoD) but in practice little came through that channel. This should have been a major source of information since the RAE possessed a very extensive library, but there was no direct access to it for industry and hence no way of knowing what they had. There were a few papers in the Warton Technical Library, which, in the absence of anything else, were studied in depth.

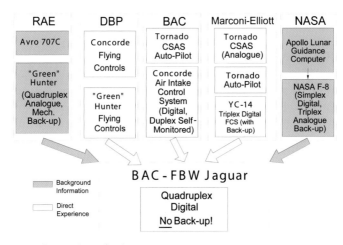

Figure 10 System Experience at Start of Main Programme

1.5   The Programme Gets Underway

In mid-1977 BAe was given the go-ahead from the MoD to design and develop a full time FBW system and subsequently to flight-test an aircraft that would demonstrate both the benefits and problems associated with Active Control Technology. A team was set up under Dave Parry for the engineering of the programme. The design engineers were seconded from their original departments for the duration of the project and located together, initially in the Jaguar Projects office, but a little later moved into 7

Hangar, where the team was conveniently situated between the test rig at one end of the building and the aircraft at the other. For a small research team this proved a very efficient way of working.

Undoubtedly much of the success of the programme was due to the leadership of Dave Parry who combined the roles of Technical and Project Manager. He had the advantage of both an aerodynamic and flight test background, together with an excellent grasp of programme management (being previously the deputy Jaguar Project Manager). He was respected at director level and as a result, although some possibly found him a bit abrasive, he did succeed in getting things done. This was important since small projects in large organisations can find it difficult to get any priority in terms of people and other resources. When Dave Parry moved on to other projects in 1981, his role was taken over by Edward Daley (previously his deputy) who saw the programme to a successful conclusion.

The Jaguar FBW aircraft was conceived from the start with the aim of investigating the practical engineering and flight clearance of a FBW aircraft. It was important that the aircraft met the performance requirements of a modern aircraft and would achieve control integrity levels similar to aircraft with conventional mechanical or hydro-mechanical controls. The programme was not intended to demonstrate the aerodynamic benefits of active control technology since as noted above these could be adequately covered by theoretical studies. However, it was intended to fly the aircraft in an unstable pitch configuration and to demonstrate a stall and spin prevention system.

The design of the flight control system assumed that a similar level of airworthiness and clearance would be required to that of a production system – no short cuts were to be taken based on it being 'only an experimental aircraft'. Therefore, it was intended to investigate the techniques of safe software and to identify those additional control procedures required for the design, testing and qualification of a high integrity fly-by-wire system. Indeed subsequent to the programme, the lessons learnt in these respects were used as the basis for the Active Controls chapter of DEF STAN 00 970[10].

As noted above the initial programme objective was the practical engineering and flight clearance of a control system meeting stringent performance and safety requirements. A further deliberate ploy was to avoid from the outset any form of backup, either mechanical or analogue. It was considered that the existence of such a backup might mean that the real design problems would be avoided because of the presence of a 'crutch'. Adopting full-time digital fly-by-wire from first flight meant tackling the airworthiness issues head-on.

The performance requirements were as follows:

• The ability to give handling qualities at least as good as a standard Jaguar

---

[10] DEF STAN 970 started life as AP970 (Air Publication 970) at the end of the First World War. It contains the requirements that must be met by service aircraft and advice on how some of the requirements may be met.

- The ability to control a longitudinal aerodynamically unstable aircraft configuration
- The ability to automatically prevent departure (stall) or loss of control (spin)

Additional objectives could be summarised as follows:

- Throughout the design, development, clearance for flight and flight-testing, the system was to be treated in all airworthiness aspects as though it were intended for production
- Special attention to be paid to resistance against electromagnetic interference and the effects of lightning

These requirements were decomposed to form top-level drivers for the system:

i.   The probability of aircraft loss as a result of electronic failures of computers, sensors or first stage actuation was not to exceed 10^{-7} per flight hour.

ii. The system was to survive any two electrical failures.

iii. The system was to survive a single electrical failure and a single hydraulic failure.

iv. Majority voting (rather than self-monitoring) was to be used as the principal means of failure detection and location.

v.   Similar software and hardware would be used in each lane i.e. dissimilarity would not be used as a counter to generic defects of design or implementation.

vi. A 'simple' actuator design was desired to avoid the need for complex and difficult to set up, hydro-mechanical voters.

Strictly speaking, requirement ii can be derived from i, since at that time typical failure rates for electronics (one flight control computer) amounted to around 10^{-3} failures per hour, a system would have to be able to survive two failures to meet the safety rate. This could be achieved by either a triplex system with a high level of self-monitoring or a quadruplex system. Because of a lack of experience in the design of self-monitoring at the electronics supplier, the easier quadruplex solution was chosen. An indirect advantage of quadruplex is the psychological feeling that it is better able to survive two failures. Similarly, long distance aircraft always used to have three or four engines, whereas today engines have become so much more reliable that long distance twins are the norm for many airlines.

For the actuators, a sextuplex or duo-triplex design was produced by Dowty Boulton Paul (DBP). This used six servo valves, the outputs of which were force summed onto the main control valve. The advantage of such a configuration is that with such a high level of redundancy, failures can be absorbed provided that there is always a majority of good lanes to overcome the failed lanes. In this instance, since the basic actuator was tandem and fed by two hydraulic supply systems, it could survive two electrical lane failures (or servo valve failures) if both hydraulic systems were available. After a hydraulic supply failure, one group of three servo valves would be lost, but the system could continue working on the remaining set and still absorb an electrical failure.

2   THE AIRCRAFT AND SYSTEM MODIFICATIONS

The aircraft selected to be the demonstrator was a standard single seat Jaguar (manufacturer's number S62, RAF serial XX765) that had already been in service with the RAF and was therefore technically 'on-loan' for the programme. It was delivered to Warton from RAF Abingdon by BAe's pilot (Eric Bucklow) on August 4th 1978. The aircraft was equipped with Mk 104 Adour engines. The team had expected the RAF to give up an old, worn out airframe and were pleasantly surprised to receive one with fairly low flying hours.

For most of the programme, the aircraft was to be located in 7 Hangar where it would be close to the development rig and project team. The first task was to remove equipment that would not be necessary on the FBW aircraft; in particular, most of the existing flight control system components such as the control rods, actuators, auto-stab etc. The stick and AJAX pitch feel system were retained but modified to suit FBW. On the standard Jaguar the AJAX feel system provides a characteristic which varies with dynamic pressure and hence airspeed. The basic objective of such feel systems, which are used on many aircraft, is to provide a natural feel whereby the force that has to be exerted on the stick increases with airspeed. Clearly, this is what happens with simple mechanical controls, as speed increases so does the amount of force needed to deflect the flying controls, and therefore it feels natural to the pilot and helps to avoid over-stressing at high speed. At the start of the programme, it was by no means obvious whether this feature would be required on a fly-by-wire aircraft and so evaluation of a simple invariable characteristic was one of the objectives. Thus as the initial base line the AJAX was fixed to provide a relatively linear simple feel (in the pitch axis). By leaving the rest of the system intact, (but isolated) it could be restored later should this have proved necessary. In practice, fixed feel remained throughout the flight test phase and led to subsequent aircraft (EAP and Typhoon) also having the advantage of simple spring feel pilot's controls.

Other equipment had to be taken out to provide room for the new equipment; this included the gun, ammunition boxes and laser designator in the nose. As an additional precaution, the high frequency radio transmitter was removed in case it caused interference to the FBW system. On standard RAF aircraft, the HF radio had a reputation for causing minor twitching through the standard Jaguar's auto stabiliser. Operationally, the lack of HF radio was unimportant for a demonstrator aircraft flying within UK airspace where VHF radio was available.

2.1   Variable Stability

Provision was made to 'destabilise' the aircraft both by means of ballast and later by the fitting of wing leading edge strakes (to move the aerodynamic centre-of-lift forward).

Provision was made to fit either forward or aft ballast. The forward ballast was located in the nose replacing the laser rangefinder and marked target seeker (LRMTS), and the ballast plus its mounting tray amounted to 75kg. Alternatively, ballast could be located at the rear of the aircraft, and here the mounting tray plus ballast weighed a maximum of 290kg, but a partial level of 194kg was used during earlier stages of the flight trials programme. The centre of gravity (c.g.) position could also be adjusted by modifying the total or sequence of use of fuel from the various tanks. Some care was needed with the extreme rear c.g. with the aircraft on the ground, not to upend the aircraft onto its tail.

2.1.1   Wing Leading Edge Strakes

To achieve the maximum required levels of aircraft instability was impossible using ballast alone. For later flight phases, the c.g. shift given by the ballast was complemented by an opposite centre of lift movement achieved by adding large leading edge strakes. Following successful wind tunnel tests, the strakes were manufactured and fitted to the aircraft mid-way through the flight trials programme. The three attachment points on the port strake were strain gauged to provide records of strake loading. The strake itself was amply stressed for 8g manoeuvres, but the changed distribution of wing loading resulted in a 5g overall clearance. Fitting of the strakes was the major configuration change from a standard Jaguar aircraft.

2.1.2   Spin Recovery Parachute

Because it was planned to carry out flight trials of the Stall Departure and Spin Prevention (SDSP) function of the FCS, a spin parachute was necessary as an alternative fit to the standard Jaguar brake parachute. This installation as designed had a combination of features previously used on Jaguar and Tornado development aircraft.

2.1.3   Electrical Power Generation

Unlike earlier conventional aeroplanes that could operate (albeit with severe restrictions) without electrical power, a fly-by-wire aircraft is utterly dependent on electrical power. This dependence on electrical power imposed demands for supply integrity much greater than that of the standard Jaguar aircraft. That requirement, coupled with increased power demands, required modification to the standard power generation system. The standard Jaguar has two engine driven alternators, providing power to two 115V AC bus bars. DC power is then produced by two transformer rectifier units (TRUs) and under normal conditions each TRU is fed from a different alternator; however, following an engine or alternator failure both TRUs may be fed from one alternator.

Overall, on the FBW aircraft, the electrical generation system had to meet the following requirements:

• The additional DC load of the FCS

• An improvement in integrity to render the risk of either momentary interrupts or total loss of electrical supply to an acceptable level (less than 10^{-7} per flight hour)

• In the event of a double engine flame out (most probably during high incidence test flying) the electrical system had to provide power to two electro-hydraulic pumps to provide hydraulic supplies until an engine re-light could be accomplished

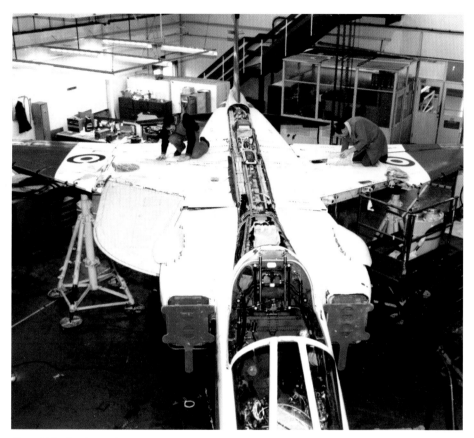

Figure 11 Strakes Conversion

The criticality of electric power led to an outline of the required system changes being prepared as early as February 1975 during the Feasibility Study[xvi]. Eventually the system was modified for FBW by the addition of a third TRU, supplying a new dedicated Flying Controls bus bar (FC). This bus bar was backed by an additional battery, of 23-ampère hour capacity. An additional 40-ampère hour battery supported bus bar P18. Bus bar P2 was supported by a 40-ampère hour battery, unchanged from standard Jaguar. Each FCS computer was supplied from two bus bars, via the power switches on the Pilot's Control and Switch Panel. Within each FCS computer, the two 28 Volt inputs were diode consolidated so as to prevent the failure of one bus bar affecting a healthy one. Furthermore, there were diodes in series with the feeds from bus bars P2 and P18; due to the volt-drop across these diodes, under normal failure-free conditions the FCS was supplied from the FC bus bar. The two electro-hydraulic pumps were connected to bus bars P18 and P2; any transients occurring during their switch-on current surge would not affect bus bar FC and therefore could have no effect on the FCS operation.

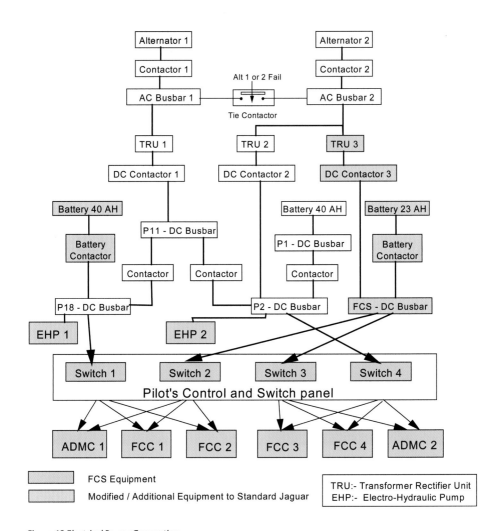

Figure 12 Electrical Power Generation

An interesting aside of the specification of the electrical power supply arose as an illustration of the danger of using standard specifications without a full understanding of the origin of the various requirements. The Jaguar power generation system was specified as meeting a British standard, BS3G100, Part 3. Now that specification included an over voltage surge of up to 80 Volts and that surge was very difficult for MAv to meet in a satisfactory manner. Later it was discovered that in reality that condition only applied to the RAF powering aircraft from ground supplies with no batteries in circuit – it was not a real case for the FBW Jaguar at all.

2.1.4   Hydraulic Power Generation

The hydraulic power generation system had to be modified because of the more demanding nature of the FBW control system. The basic Jaguar has a 3000 psi duplex system, and this was modified by fitting higher flow rate pumps, Sperry Vickers type PV3-115-1GB1, of 14.6 gallons per minute capacity to each system. The pipe runs to the taileron and rudder actuators were increased in bore, to reduce pressure losses at the higher flow rates of the FBW actuators.

To protect the aircraft in the event of short-term loss of both engine driven pumps, two electro-hydraulic pumps (EHPs) were fitted. These were sized to cope with the hydraulic demands in the event of a double engine flame out occurring during high incidence flight trials, and to provide a safe ejection platform in the event of a double engine failure when the aircraft was in an aerodynamically unstable configuration. The new pumps fitted were Sperry Vickers type MPEV3-011-GB11, with a flow rate of 3.3 gallons per minute. This reduced flow rate (compared to the engine driven pumps) was satisfactory for the expected conditions of low control surface activity for spin recovery or stabilisation. Operation of these EHPs was under pilot control rather than automatically via low-pressure switches.

Notwithstanding that the EHPs were only intended for short time use, their reduced flow capability resulted in an interesting conversation in one of the pre-flight briefings when the aircraft was to be flown in the most aerodynamically unstable configuration. It was pointed out that if operating on EHPs alone, there would be insufficient flow capability to both control the aircraft and to lower the undercarriage at the same time. As the Jaguar was prohibited from 'belly landing', the Airworthiness representative insisted that in this event the procedure would be to eject and abandon the aircraft. The pilot's response was direct and straightforward 'B…r the procedure, I'm not going to abandon a flying aircraft, in particular a one-off such as this one. I would declare a Mayday to divert to RAF Valley, request a blanket of foam on the runway and belly-land'. The Airworthiness man could only splutter indignantly. Fortunately, this scenario was never put to the test.

2.1.5   Air Conditioning

The normal Jaguar air conditioning system was retained but with additional ducts to feed cooling air to the FCS computers. Cooling of electronics is always important and for flight control computers especially so. Testing was undertaken during system qualification to ensure that the computers would operate for a short time without cooling; the specification required a minimum of 15 minutes, though in practice they would probably last considerably longer. Consequently, to be safe, the pilot was instructed to land within 15 minutes of an air conditioning failure.

It is of interest to note that some avionics incorporates thermal cut-outs to minimise the risk of damage should the cooling air supply fail; such features are not permitted in flight controls – the safety of the aircraft and pilot are much more important than reduced equipment life.

3   SYSTEM DESIGN

The FCS was designed primarily to have a basic dual fault survival capability, but in reality it was the design of the actuators that had a deciding influence in the overall system configuration. With an essentially quadruplex set of Flight Control Computers (FCCs), it was necessary to derive two additional lanes to drive the six-input actuators. The problem was how to interface four FCCs with each of the six lane first stage actuators in such a way that one or two FCC failures could not propagate to more than two lanes of the six lane actuators. The solution which was adopted was to interface the four FCCs on a one-to-one basis with four out of the six lanes of each first stage actuator, and to drive the remaining two lanes of each first stage actuator with independently voted versions of the FCC output drive signals. These two additional voting nodes required two further computers, each with appropriate segregation of data transmission and power supplies etc., in order to eliminate any possibility of inter-lane fault propagation between the six parallel lanes. This is shown in the following figure.

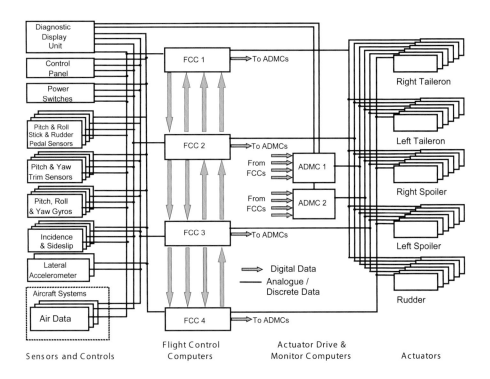

Figure 13 Overall System Design

Thus in detail the system had four independent computing lanes each providing a single output to each of the five force summing actuators. In order to provide six outputs to the duo-triplex actuators two further drive outputs were generated by the Actuator Drive and Monitor Computers (ADMCs). These two analogue computers received actuator position error commands from the four FCCs via the serial digital links. The cross lane digital data transmission system was required for input sensor data cross-comparison by the digital computers, the transfer of input data from those sensors of less than quadruplex redundancy, the transfer of actuator inner loop position demand data to the ADMCs for lanes 5 and 6, and the transfer of some failure status information to the ADMCs.

All primary sensors were quadruplex to match the computing redundancy level. These included the pitch, roll and yaw gyros, pilot's control position sensors (pitch and roll stick, rudder pedals and trim). Control panel switches (which provided mode selection, etc.) and undercarriage lever position were also quadruplex. Other sensors, classified as 'non-essential' were provided at a lesser level of redundancy. In particular, pitot/static data was triplex, incidence and sideslip pseudo triplex; the lateral accelerometer, airbrake and flap positions, duplex.

3.1   Flight Control Computer (FCC)

Figure 14 The Flight Control Computer

The four FCCs were identical and interchangeable. Since, however, they had to interface with different sensors depending on their lane position, they had to know their lane number as installed in the aircraft. To that end, links in the aircraft wiring were used to identify each lane to its software. Each FCC was housed in a ¾ ATR short case containing 24 printed circuit modules and a power supply unit. The front of the unit carried eight connectors, six for aircraft services and two for ground test purposes. Cooling of the computer was by air forced directly across the surface of the modules and by conduction of heat via 'thermal ladders' to the chassis of the computer. It should be noted that more modern avionics are generally indirectly cooled via a 'cold wall' to prevent contamination of the electronics by dirt or water in the cooling air.

The electronic modules in the FCC performed four main functions:

- Interfacing with sensors
- Outputs to actuation
- Cross-lane data transmission and reception
- The digital processor, implementing the control laws, voting, mode selection, signal selection, failure management and Built in Test (BIT)

The main digital processor (i.e. the computer proper) was based on a 16-bit Harvard architecture, implemented using 'bit slice' technology. The instruction set was optimised for the flight control task, and was micro-coded in Programmable Read Only Memories (PROMs); average instruction time was 1.59μs. The main FCC program was also stored in PROMs; 28K instructions could be stored. A further 2K of constants were stored in the data store, and a 4K scratch pad provided working storage for 16 bit and 1 bit information. The instruction set was as follows:

MNEMONIC	GENERAL DESCRIPTION	TIME μs
MOD	Modify address field of next instruction	2.25
ADD	Add data to accumulator	0.5
NAD	Negate accumulator and add data	0.79
STE	Store extension register in data location	1.0
LDA	Load accumulator with data	0.5
STA	Store accumulator in data location	1.0
AND	Logical AND accumulator with data	0.5
RST	Delay master reset	0.5
JMP	Unconditional relative jump	2.0
JNE	Jump relative if accumulator negative	2.0
IOR	Logical inclusive OR accumulator with data	1.75
CALL RETURN	Sub-routine entry/exit	1.75

MNEMONIC	GENERAL DESCRIPTION	TIME μs
MUL	Multiply accumulator by data – result in accumulator and extension register	5.0
DIV	Divide accumulator and extension register by data – result in accumulator	5.75
SHL	Arithmetic shift left by 'n'	1.0 + 0.25n
SHR	Arithmetic shift right by 'n'	1.0 + 0.25n
CON	Load accumulator with next program store word	1.0
SUM	Sum program store location	1.5

The interface modules converted the analogue signals from the sensors; this could take the form of a DC voltage (e.g. from a stick position sensor), an AC signal from a Linear Variable Differential Transformer (LVDT) (used to measure actuator position), or a switched voltage. Direct memory access was used to load information into the computer RAM i.e. no interrupts were necessary. Similarly, the outputs of the control laws, in the form of surface position errors, were read from the scratch pad and following digital-to-analogue conversion sent to the servo drive modules. There were five servo-drive amplifiers, one per actuator. The analogue control valve position signal was summed with surface position error on the latter modules, thus generating the servo valve demand.

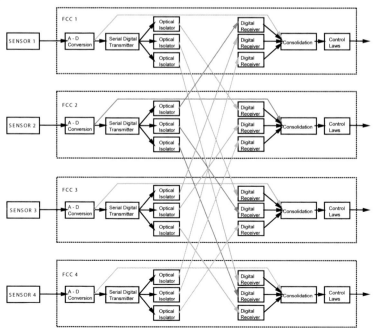

Figure 15 Sensor Data Exchange and Consolidation (Voting)

Information was transmitted between the FCCs and from the FCCs to the ADMCs via serial digital data links at a data rate of 503,000 bits per second; each word comprising 32 bits. A single transmitter in each FCC drove optical isolators, one per lane, and so fed the other computers in the system. The object was to ensure complete electrical isolation between lanes, thereby preventing fault propagation between lanes in the event of a catastrophic FCC failure or other problems such as the aircraft being struck by lightning. An important aspect of the transmission system design was to avoid the possibility of misinformation in the event of a computer fault[11]. The links were unidirectional and the transmitting computer simply 'stuffed' its data onto the link and did not depend at all on the receiving FCC – if the receiving FCC failed, it could not affect the transmitting FCC in any way whatsoever. In each receiving FCC, the data transmitted from the other three FCCs was decoded and routed to the processor memory by direct memory access. The main initial task was to vote on incoming data from the various sensors.

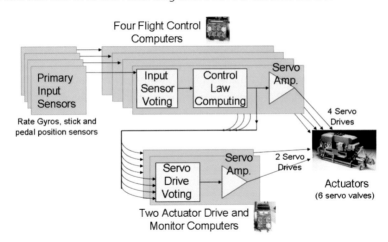

Figure 16 Simplified System Diagram

3.1.1   Build Stages 'A', 'B' and 'C'

In comparison with later projects, (such as EAP) the Jaguar was fairly well provided with hardware. In part, this was to take account of anticipated problems and the gradual maturing of the design through system development at the suppliers.

The first hardware to be delivered was intended for use only in a laboratory (rig) environment being constructed as standard 19-inch racks. There was one set of 'A' models (i.e. four computers and two ADMCs). It was also intended that this version of the FCCs should have an easily re-programmable memory to take account of software development. The original suggestion was that this could have been provided by a magnetic core store[12]; however, even by the middle seventies, core was becoming

---

[11] As postulated by Dr Meredith of Smiths Industries during the Feasibility Study, see reference x.
[12] The original Space Shuttle computers (IBM AP101s) used core store.

obsolescent and an alternative semiconductor store was proposed by MAv. This part of the system (known to all as the 'lab ram') was bought in as standard commercial equipment. In practice, and despite many weeks of hard work by Robin Heaps (on secondment to Warton from MAv Rochester), the lab ram never worked satisfactorily and so the 'A' models had to use erasable programmable read only memories.

'B' models were identical in form with the eventual aircraft units but not cleared for flight (and hence bore a red band). The Jaguar project had one set of 'B' models. 'C' models formed the basis of the flight programme in that they were fully cleared for flight (given the necessary paperwork) Jaguar had two sets of 'C' models to give maximum flexibility and to cover defects and repairs without affecting the flight test trials. In practice, the reliability of the FCCs was very good and was a credit to the suppliers. Both the 'B' and 'C' models used fusible link programmable read only memories (PROMs). These had the advantage that the likelihood of corruption were very remote, but the disadvantage that they had to be thrown away if a change was required. A problem did occur with the PROMs supplied from one manufacturer in that the fuses, having been blown tended to migrate and repair themselves. Naturally these were not used for aircraft equipment, but it is revealing that a technology proven by one supplier may not automatically be satisfactory when manufactured by another.

It is also of interest that the steady maturing of memory technology meant that by the time EAP was ready to fly (in 1986), erasable devices, considered suitable only for 'A' models on the Jaguar, were cleared for flight from the start of that programme.

3.2   Actuator Drive And Monitor Computer (ADMC)

The ADMC was basically an analogue computer having two main functions:

- Generation of fifth and sixth actuator drive lanes

- Collation of failure information from the FCCs. This was then used to drive the warning lamps in the cockpit. They also drove the Diagnostic Display Unit located in the port undercarriage bay

Each ADMC consisted of a ½ ATR short case containing its own power supply unit and with space for 16 printed circuit modules (13 used and 3 spare). Four connectors were mounted on the front of the unit; three carried aircraft services, and the fourth was for ground test use.

Figure 17 Actuator Drive and Monitor Computer

There were four digital receivers in each ADMC which received data from all four FCCs. Contained within this data stream was the FCCs' actuator control valve demands, these were decoded and converted to analogue signals, and then passed to analogue Voter-Monitor circuits, one per actuator drive. These circuits calculated an average of the four inputs, and so performed comparisons to look for disparities between the inputs. Any input which exceeded the failure threshold for a defined time was disconnected and the appropriate warning given. A second failure would then result in disconnection of that lane as well. The outputs of the averaging circuits were then fed to the servo amplifiers. Control valve demand was summed with the demodulated inner loop position signal, and a current output to drive the actuator servo valves generated.

Also present on the data streams from the FCCs were discrete words containing information on the status of each FCC and its sensors. These data, collated by logic in the ADMCs, were used to generate failure warnings to the pilot, displayed both on the FCS Pilot's Control Panel and via the Central Warning Panel to generate an audio alert. Information in the FCCs' Failure Identification Table (FIT) was transmitted to the ADMCs. ADMC2 had an interface with the numeric display on the DDU for interrogation by the ground crew post flight.

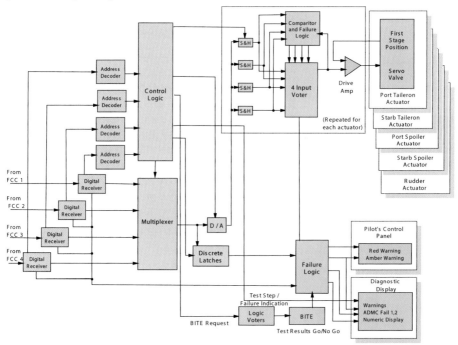

Figure 18 ADMC Functional Diagram

3.3   Rate Gyro Units (RGU)

Figure 19 The Quadruplex Rate Gyro Unit

There were three RGUs, one each for pitch, roll and yaw. They were identical apart from the scaling of their output signals, a wider range being required for roll rate. Each contained four gyroscopes and associated electronics, these being housed in compartments featuring mechanical and electrical isolation between each lane. They interfaced on a lane-by-lane basis with the FCCs and each FCC provided DC power to its own gyros, and received the rate signal as simple analogue values. The gyros were tested before flight (during the pre-flight check) by means of a torquer circuit. In flight, the primary means of fault detection was by comparison monitoring between lanes, but in addition, a discrete signal was used to indicate internally detected failures through a wheel speed monitor. This latter check was intended to minimise the risk of two sequential faults to zero rate leading to a two-versus-two condition. This problem might arise because during cruise the outputs from the gyros would naturally be close to zero (i.e. zero aircraft rates) for a prolonged period. Under these conditions, should two gyros fail (to zero output, the most likely failure) then when the aircraft commenced to manoeuvre then these two lanes would continue to give zero and the other two the real value. Such a two versus two condition cannot be resolved by simple voters and was therefore a potential safety critical condition. Hence, it was important to minimise the likelihood of such conditions and then make an assessment based on time at risk during which such failures might occur. This was done within MAv's assessment and the failure rate estimated as 10.69 ppmh (parts per million hours). A critical condition would arise only if a second similar failure were to occur. The overall probability of this occurring was estimated as 2.06×10^{-9} per hour, an entirely acceptable risk. This calculation was one of many that were carried out within the Integrity Assessment[xvii], and is given here as an example of the detail and care required to clear the system for flight.

The rate gyros were housed in simple boxes to the full available space envelope; as purely prototype equipment, low cost was more important than minimum size. Some problems were initially experienced with build quality – one box was found to rattle, a heat sink had come loose from a transistor!

In addition, the rear of one card was found to be scraping the wall of the box and only the conformal coating[13] prevented short circuits. Other difficulties were experienced with electrical noise, which was found to originate in the elapsed time indicators. Once these problems were overcome, the units were found to be perfectly satisfactory. No in-flight failures or other defects arose to the end of the flight test programme.

3.4   Pilot's Control And Switch Panel (PCSP)

The following controls and indicators were provided on this panel:

- Four power switches: these controlled the 28 Volt supplies from three aircraft bus bars to the six FCS computers. The supplies were routed in such a way that operation of these switches in a defined sequence during PFC would test the 28 Volt consolidation diodes in each computer

- Status/Reset indicator/button: this was provided with amber and red captions to indicate FCS status (amber for single failures, red for double). When the aircraft was in the air, it could be pressed to attempt to reset a first failure

- BIT Button: this had green and amber captions used by the PFC. Apart from initiating pre-flight test, it was also pressed at various points during pilot participation in the PFC

- Autopilot mode selection buttons: these were provisioned for an autopilot, but the autopilot control laws were never implemented in the FCC software

- Sensor failure warning captions: to indicate Pitot-Static, Incidence/Sideslip, Weight-on-Wheels (labelled Lateral Acceleration) or Airbrake/Flap failure

- Gain switch: to enable selection of up to three sets of control laws

The PCSP was difficult to manufacture because of the need to provide interfaces with all four lanes yet still maintain adequate segregation. The lack of space also meant that it was difficult to fit adequately rated power switches with the result that they tended to weld themselves shut on the initial current inrush when the equipment was switched on; this was due to the need for large value capacitors to absorb the transient surge specified in BS3G100 (see section 2.1.3). Workarounds were found by leaving the switches 'on' and using the aircraft circuit breakers to power the system.

3.5   Triplex Transducer

Static and Pitot-static pressures were measured by the Jaguar Triplex Transducer Unit (JTTU), an item based on the prototype Tornado transducer unit. The JTTU contained three pairs of pressure transducers, each pair supplying static (altitude) and pitot-static (airspeed) data to one of the FCCs (either 1, 2 or 3). These transducers were connected pneumatically to three independent pitot pressure sources (from the nose probe and the two fuselage mounted pitot-static probes) and three static pressure sources (two from the nose probe and one from the fuselage mounted probes, with left and right

---

[13] Conformal coating is a moisture proof varnish used to protect printed circuit cards from dampness and other contaminants.

Figure 20
Pilot's Control and
Switch Panel

static tappings averaged (pneumatically) to reduce the effect of sideslip. Since this was essentially the same as the standard Jaguar, existing calibration data applied equally to the FBW Jaguar.

The pressure transducers were very simple analogue devices; essentially a bellows arrangement driving a potentiometer with the latter excited by a +/- 12 Volt supply from the FCCs. No problems were experienced with the operation of this equipment during the Jaguar programme.

3.6   Incidence And Sideslip

The standard Jaguar has a single incidence probe to drive a cockpit instrument. Initial thoughts for FBW were to add a second incidence probe (i.e. a duplex system) to enable fault detection by cross-comparison. However, during 1975, a meeting was held with MBB in Munich and the Germans explained that for their experimental FBW Starfighter, they were going to use four probes arranged around the front fuselage over 120° so that each probe would pick up a mixture of incidence and sideslip. Hence, by the straightforward application of simultaneous equations they were able to derive what amounted to a triplex version of the two prime parameters of incidence and sideslip. It was therefore decided to try a similar system on the FBW Jaguar.

The flat underside of the Jaguar nose and the sharp corners of the cross-section precluded spreading the probes over 120° on the Jaguar. Two were mounted on the underside of the nose and two on the sides. Since it was by no means certain that this arrangement would be satisfactory, it was decided to test the proposed probe installation on a Jaguar development aircraft (S1) prior to the fly-by-wire programme. Testing demonstrated that the arrangement was just about satisfactory, though not ideal owing to the less

than ideal shape of the Jaguar nose. Never-the-less installation went ahead on the FBW Jaguar and worked sufficiently well to be used on the follow on aircraft, namely EAP and Typhoon, and eventually a similar arrangement even found employment on the Nimrod MRA4.

Figure 21 shows the nose of the Jaguar together with three of the four incidence/sideslip probes (identified by their ground covers and flags). Also to be seen is one of the pitot/static probes with a yellow ground cover.

Figure 21 Installation of the Incidence and Sideslip Probes

The control laws use incidence and sideslip for two main reasons. Firstly, to provide good handling in part by restoring 'speed stability'. A pure pitch rate command system tries to hold aircraft attitude constant as speed changes, a more natural expectation by pilots is for the aircraft incidence to change in response to speed changes. This characteristic can be restored by using incidence feedback and was provided on all issues of the controls apart from the rate demand system used for initial flying. Secondly, to enable incidence to be limited automatically to a safe value ('carefree handling'), thus preventing either stalling or spinning, both of which are most undesirable on a Jaguar. Sideslip feedback improves directional stability, i.e. it has a similar effect to the 'weather cock' effect of the fin.

Experience with the sensors was generally good, but one flight had to be aborted as a result of a 'sensor' failure caption being displayed on take-off. This was found to be due to a probe with excessive friction not lining up as speed increased. It had in fact been 'twiddled' by a test engineer showing guests around the aircraft before flight and left out of line. Even so, this was a real defect and more precise testing of probe friction was made thereafter as part of ground pre-flight checks.

3.7   Quadruplex Position Sensor (QPS)

The position of the pilot's flying controls was measured by means of a set of Quadruplex Position Sensors. Each inceptor (pitch stick, roll stick, rudder pedals, pitch trim actuator position and lateral trim) was attached to a unit containing a set of plastic film potentiometers. Although part of the MAv contract, these sensors were actually designed and built by Penny and Giles Ltd. This meant that a couple of progress meetings and design reviews were held at Penny and Giles' facility at Blackwood in Gwent

Figure 22 Quadruplex Position Sensor (Author)

The Jaguar safety requirements stressed that no single failure should result in aircraft loss, and so the design of parts that were inherently common to all four lanes needed careful consideration. It was accepted that the input shaft had to be common, but it was designed to be of more than adequate strength and x-rayed for flaws. The input bearing was duplex comprising a main ball bearing and backup plain bearing. The input shaft drove the four potentiometers through sun and planet gears and tests were undertaken to show that a broken tooth would not result in a jam.

3.8   Airbrake and Flap Angle

During system definition, consideration was given to measuring airbrake and flap angle. This was because deployment of these secondary-flying surfaces tends to give rise to unwanted pitch disturbances and there was a desire to have them automatically suppressed by the flight control system. However, because the aircraft could continue flying without such compensation, there was no need for full quadruplex sensors, duplex was adequate so as to at least allow automatic failure detection.

A simple rotary position transducer was mounted inside the starboard airbrake bay to measure airbrake angle. This unit contained two wire wound potentiometers to provide airbrake position to FCCs numbers 3 and 4.

FCCs 3 and 4 also obtained flap angle from a pair of potentiometers in the flap limit switch assembly (end of travel unit), located on the flap drive circuit in the port wing.

As with other non-quadruplex sensors, digitised parameters were passed between FCCs via the digital data links. Both airbrake angle and flap angle were expected to be used by the control laws to prevent undesirable pitch changes as these surfaces moved. In practice, it was found that the pitch rate feedback alone virtually wiped out trim changes – indeed with an early version of the control laws, pitching moment compensation was too powerful and induced a trim change in the opposite sense.

3.9   Undercarriage Selection

On a FBW aircraft, it is desirable to be able to schedule the control laws (i.e. to vary the gains) for take-off and landing, as opposed to up-and-away flying. A convenient way of achieving this automatically is by using the position of the undercarriage selection lever. On the FBW Jaguar, a second four-pole switch unit was mechanically linked to the existing U/C selection lever by using the equipment designed for the two seat aircraft, which of course requires a link between the cockpits. Because of the criticality of U/C position, this information was fed to all four FCCs.

In practice it was discovered that simply using another Jaguar U/C switch had its limitations and surprises. On flight 13, which was the last of the initial test flights with issue one control laws, a 'Red Warning' occurred when the aircraft was on final approach for landing. Happily, the pilot carried on and made a successful landing. Naturally, a rapid investigation was carried out and by the afternoon it had been discovered that the problem was caused by the design of the U/C switch. In the Jaguar switch mechanism, a cam operated two pairs of micro switches and in practice, if the U/C selection lever was moved slowly, the signal to the computers could change one lane at a time, thus triggering the failure logic. This problem should have been found on the rig, but unfortunately, when it was being equipped, there was a shortage of true Jaguar U/C switches and an ex-Lightning unit was used. This went straight into the project 'lessons learnt' - always use actual aircraft components (and moreover for the right aircraft) on the rig.

3.10 Undercarriage 'Weight-On-Wheels'

Two micro switches on each of the two main undercarriage oleos provided a 'weight on wheels' signal. These were wired to two of the four FCCs and the two ADMCs, each switch supplying a single computer. In practice, only having a duplex 'weight on wheels' feed to the FCCs was found a distinct disadvantage and it was recommended that future FBW systems should have full quadruplex 'weight-on-wheels' signals.

Weight-on-wheels is perhaps the most underrated parameter on any aircraft as it controls many systems on both civil and military aeroplanes. It is also very difficult to provide it with the necessary level of integrity, in part because the reliability of the 'weight on wheels' signal ultimately depends on the correct extension of the leg oleo. If the oleo fails to extend properly on take-off then no weight-off-wheels signal will be sent to the flight control computers. Now if this signal is safety critical (as it frequently is on unstable aircraft), then other measures may be necessary to detect take-off (e.g. a combination of airspeed and rotation/incidence). This was not done on the Jaguar, but was found necessary on EAP and Typhoon.

3.11 Central Warning Panel (CWP)

In the event of a failure being detected by monitoring within the FCS, then the pilot would be alerted through the existing Central Warning Panel (CWP), as this included both a visual attention getter and audible warning to attract the pilot's attention. To provide space for the FCS warnings, it was fortunate that the original CWP had two spare captions, and that several standard Jaguar captions were unnecessary on the FBW aircraft, namely the 'STAB1', 'DIFF' and 'AJAX' captions (the associated systems having been removed from the FBW aircraft).

For the FBW aircraft the new captions consisted of three amber and two red warnings. The amber warnings were 'TR3', signifying a power supply failure by the new (extra) transformer/rectifier unit feeding the flight control system bus bar. Amber 'FCS1' indicated a first failure in the FCCs, ADMCs or quadruplex sensors, and amber 'SENSOR' loss of a secondary sensor (air data, lateral acceleration, incidence/sideslip or airbrake/flap position). The new red CWP captions were 'FCS' indicating a second, similar failure in the FCCs, ADMCs or quadruplex sensors, and 'A/PILOT', warning of an autopilot failure. The latter warning was not used as the autopilot software was considered to be of low priority and never implemented.

The 'FCS', 'SENSOR' and 'A/PILOT' warnings were generated by the ADMCs, either ADMC being capable of driving the caption; thus a single failure could not cause loss of the ability to display failures. The 'SENSOR' caption flashed for six seconds after each failure before becoming steady. This was because multiple sensor failures were a possibility, and it was necessary to be able to alert the pilot in each case. The actual secondary sensor failures could then be identified on the Pilot's Control Panel.

The Central Warning Panel was standard in all other respects, except for the 'BAT' caption, which was renamed 'CONTAC'. This signalled a fault in the electrical generation or battery charging system.

3.12 Diagnostic Display Unit (DDU)

Figure 23 The Diagnostic Display Unit

This unit was mounted in the port undercarriage bay, for observation and interrogation by the ground crew. It provided status information during the PFC and after flight in the event of a failure being detected by the in-flight failure monitoring. A numeric display indicated the detailed nature of FCC faults stored in the Failure Identification Table (FIT). Multiple fault codes were read by repeated pressing of the read button. Simple warning lamps indicated a fault in an ADMC as they were essentially dumb boxes.

3.13   Built In Test (BIT)

To achieve the integrity requirements of the FCS involved thorough testing before and during flight, to minimise the time at risk during which a dormant fault can exist. The BIT tests all the elements of the FCS for correct function, including tests of system redundancy and failure management. It should be noted that the BIT did not verify the operational functionality of the software within the FCCs; this was a task for the FCS rig, and was undertaken as part of clearance of the software for flight.

BIT consisted of three distinct areas; In-flight tests, Pre-Flight Check and First Line Check.

In-flight testing could then be subdivided into two areas:

• Signal monitoring and selection, which form a fundamental part of the system architecture
• Specific tests on particular system functions or areas of hardware

As noted earlier, each FCC had available all lanes of sensor data. These were compared in the voter-monitor software, and if a disparity existed for a defined time, the defective lane was deemed to have failed and was switched out of the system. The voter-monitors continuously calculated consolidated values for each input parameter, using an algorithm appropriate for the particular sensor. Defective lanes were removed from this calculation as and when a failure was detected. Voter-monitors were provided for the quadruplex primary sensors and feedbacks, whilst triplex voter-monitors processed the air data signals, and duplex voter-monitors for the flap and airbrake signals. There were also discrete voter-monitors to handle switched inputs, such as weight-on-wheels or gain switch position. The voter-monitors signalled detection of a failure to the pilot via the cockpit warning lamps, and set an appropriate code in the FIT for interrogation on the DDU after flight.

Self-monitoring was carried out in flight to check the operation of the processor, its memory and the interface modules of the FCC. The in-flight checks comprised:

• Tests of correct execution of all instructions
• Cross-lane check of program and constant store locations
• Check of digital-analogue and analogue-digital conversions
• Checks on digital data transmission and reception
• Test of gyro unit failure discretes
• Overflow monitor

Pre-flight Check was, as its name implies, a comprehensive test of the system carried out prior to flight. The objective was to reduce the time at risk as a result of any dormant failures (i.e. those failures not detectable by the in-flight monitoring) to the duration of a flight, typically 1 hour. There were two phases to PFC - automatic checks and those requiring pilot participation. Successful completion of these checks was required before the system entered Flight Resident Software (FRS) enabling the control laws to be executed. To prevent the accidental operation of PFC in the air, an interlock was fitted such that PFC could only be started with weight-on-wheels. It was initiated by powering the system, raising the BITE press button cover guard and operating the button. The following automatic checks were then carried out:

- Computer functions check
- Program and Constant Store cyclic redundancy check
- Scratch pad read/write check (all locations)
- Weight-on-wheels discrete check
- Digital transmitter/receiver failure detection checks
- Discrete outputs check
- Discrete inputs check
- D-A/A-D loop check
- Analogue inputs check
- Overflow protection check
- Checkword monitor check
- Gyro and Accelerometer torquing
- Autotrim check
- Lane coding check

Whilst these checks were being carried out under the control of the FCC software, the ADMCs concurrently ran their own Built-in-Tests. Due to the analogue nature of the ADMCs, the outcome was restricted to a simple 'go' or a 'no go', indicating whether the check had passed or not, whereas a failure of an FCC could be fully identified by an input to the Failure Identification Table (FIT).

The second phase of PFC required the participation of the pilot. The tests involved were as follows:

- 28 Volt supply consolidation
- Pitch, roll and yaw stick/pedal QPS tracking
- Yaw trim QPS tracking
- Spin Recovery and Training Mode switch tests

Following these tests, the actuators were tested for tracking of the outer loop position transducers and for correct dynamic performance of the inner loops, including servo valves and control valve position transducers. A fault in any of the six inner loops was detected by this test. Such was the power of actuator BIT that one defect, a partially blocked servo valve nozzle, was found by the PFC and not by off-aircraft testing at Warton. The affected unit had to be returned to DBP for disassembly to locate the problem.

First Line Check was an optional phase of testing, involving ground crew participation, to check certain non-safety critical aspects of the system. These were as follows:

- Check of the DDU operation
- Check of autopilot mode selection buttons on the Pilot's Control and Switch Panel
- Check of Air Data and Incidence/Sideslip probes
- Check of Airbrake and Flap position sensors
- Check of sensor warning captions on the PCSP

3.14 Actuation

Figure 24 FBW Jaguar Taileron Actuator

Each of the five primary flight control surfaces (two spoilers, two tailerons and rudder) had a hydraulic actuator designed and supplied by Dowty Boulton Paul.

The design of the actuators was new and original to meet both the performance and safety requirements of the Jaguar whilst avoiding the complexity of those used on Tornado. On the Tornado, the actuators have to switch-out failed electrical lanes by means of a hydro-mechanical voter, and after a second electrical failure, revert to mechanical mode (direct link from the pilot's stick). On the Jaguar, by designing the actuators to absorb failures, there was no need for mechanical contrivances to vote on failed inputs and as the aircraft was intended to be full-time fly-by-wire, mechanical reversion was not necessary. This significantly reduced actuator complexity and weight, whilst also eliminating control rods and levers from the aircraft itself, very helpful in reducing weight. In addition, on the standard Jaguar, there was a control problem in that spurious inputs were introduced as a result of fuselage bending, which was entirely avoided by fly-by-wire.

Each actuator consisted of a tandem ram (i.e. effectively two actuators in-line on a common output shaft) so as to survive the failure of one of the aircraft's hydraulic supplies. In respect of the spoilers and rudder, the replacement FBW actuators had similar thrust characteristics to those of the standard Jaguar, but in the case of the tailerons, it was necessary to double the thrust so that the minimum requirement would be met on a single hydraulic system. This was necessary because on an unstable aircraft control would be lost if the actuator were to sink under air loads. For comparison, on a stable aircraft this condition would only result in the desired pitch rate not being achieved.

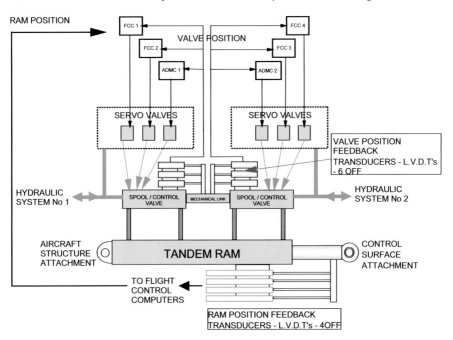

Figure 25 Actuator Schematic

Each Powered Flying Control Unit (PFCU) had three constituent stages:

- Six electro-hydraulic servo valves (EHSVs); each with its own electrical winding supplied from one of the six lanes of electronics (four from the FCCs and two from the ADMCs). The EHSVs were arranged in two banks of three, each bank being fed from one of the two aircraft hydraulic supplies. Each EHSV supplied oil to a pair of pistons that acted upon a force-summing flange also referred to as the first stage actuator

- The first stage actuator: this consisted of two spool valves, each fed from one of the hydraulic supplies. The two control valves were mechanically linked, and moved together in response to the demands of the six EHSVs, averaged by the force-summing arrangement. Six Linear Variable Differential Transformers (LVDTs) were mounted on the control valve assembly to pick off Control Valve position, which was fed back to the six inner loop servo amplifiers to close the inner loops

- The two control valves supplied hydraulic oil to two halves of a tandem ram (one mechanical forging), the output rod of which was connected to the surface-operating arm

The two halves of the actuator were therefore mechanically linked, but independent in terms of the hydraulic supplies. Each 'half' actuator had to generate sufficient thrust to control the aircraft after total loss of one hydraulic system; this required the taileron jacks to be doubled in thrust compared with the standard Jaguar. The arrangement of force-summing the output of the EHSVs provided excellent failure absorption; two of the six EHSVs, or their lanes of electronics, could fail, and the remaining four lanes could correctly control the actuator. The lane failures might take any form: null, hard-over or oscillatory.

The design also took account of a hydraulic systems failure. This left half an actuator with three servo valves, following which one of the three remaining EHSVs or drives could fail and then would be overpowered by the other two. This failure absorption approach had the advantage of minimising transients on actuator output, and the potential problem of nuisance disconnects did not arise. Its chief disadvantage was the need for six well matched servo valves and six lanes of drive electronics. Each group of position transducers (six valve position and four main ram) had to be tightly matched and this was a novel requirement at the time for LVDTs. Exceptionally, DBP decided to undertake the design in house rather than sub-contract it.

DBP also built a number of test sets for the actuators that had to simulate the digital control loops of the Flight Control Computers, again a new development, although as insurance they also built analogue equipment for back-up and comparison. The digital test sets used an 8-bit microprocessor (the 8085) that had to work with double length arithmetic to simulate the 16-bit FCC. In fact its task was made even more demanding because the FCC used some double length arithmetic (32-bit) in digital filters, and to correctly simulate this the test set had a quadruple length multiplication subroutine in software.

The actuators were subjected to extensive performance testing, in both normal and failure states. These tests verified performance in respect of:

- Frequency response
- Small amplitude (resolution)
- Hysteresis
- Impedance
- Failure transients

This involved work both at Dowty Boulton Paul and on the BAe systems rig. As originally designed, the actuators were equipped with dynamic leak valves (intended to improve stability), which were similar to those used by DBP on their Concorde actuators. During early testing at Warton, the test engineers became very frustrated owing to a complete lack of consistency between test runs; some were good and some very poor. It turned out that this inconsistent performance was due to whether the dynamic leak valve had been 'cracked open' or not at the start of a run. Consequently, prior to final qualification testing, the dynamic leak valves were removed and actuator performance found to be fully acceptable in their absence.

Following flying with Issue 1 software, the taileron actuator first stage valve ports were modified from a recto-trapezoidal shape to a trapezoidal shape. This also involved extensive repeat performance response testing on the BAe test rig. Impedance testing[14] of the actuators originally took place at DBP; following the valve port modification to the taileron actuator, repeat impedance testing was carried out by BAe.

Endurance testing of the actuators (by DBP) provided a flight clearance of 1000 hours, more than sufficient for any likely flight test programme.

3.15 Software

The software in the Flight Control Computers had the following major functions:
* Executive
* Synchronisation
* Data Management
* Signal Selection and Consolidation
* Control Laws
* Failure Identification and Management
* Built-in-test Functions

The software was divided into modules and these were then grouped to form frames, which were called at predetermined rates by the executive to perform the tasks listed above. There were thirty-two minor frames, each of which lasted 2.5ms. Filters and integrators require an accurate time reference and so the 2.5ms frames were defined by a hardware master reset signal.

The functional components of the software were segregated into defined areas of store in order to minimise the effect of a modification to the program structure, and this had the advantage of minimising the number of Programmable Read Only Memories (PROMs) that had to be changed to effect the change. The software was structured so that each frame was called as a series of link modules; groups of modules that needed to be called

---

[14] Impedance testing involves back driving an actuator to discover how 'stiff' it is. A powerful electric actuator was used for this purpose when these tests were performed at Warton. This is recalled by the engineers concerned for being extremely noisy, even penetrating thick brick walls into adjacent offices.

at the same time and in the same frame were linked together. This improved program visibility and simplified the testing of the software. A single call to a proven link module replaced a sequence of calls to individual modules. Individual modules were defined to perform one basic function, with a minimum of module interaction. This maintained the visibility, and hence the integrity. The modules were typically kept to a maximum of 50 words of program store. Each module was designed to have only one entry and one exit point, and all the computing paths were constrained to move in a forward direction, of increasing program sequence count.

In the late 1970s, compilers were not considered to have sufficient integrity for safety critical software and in addition, owing to the limited computer resources available, the resulting inefficiencies in terms of speed and computer memory were not acceptable. As a result, programming was a labour intensive operation carried out by hand in assembler code (with some assistance from a macro-assembler). However, a high level language (FORTRAN) was used to define the control law software requirements in an unambiguous manner.

Initially the facilities at Rochester for software production were extremely limited and used an Elliott 905 computer. This was a mid-sixties design with paper tape input and output, an 18 bit word length and only 8K words memory. Later this was improved by the purchase of a Nova minicomputer, but final program assembly and verification used the trusted 905. A 905 was also supplied to Warton for software changes and testing. For those interested in computer history, an Elliott 905 computer can be seen at the National Museum of Computing at Bletchley Park.

With the software being assembled on numerous paper tapes and then into the PROMs, thought was given to ensuring that the actual software as implemented in the FCC was as intended by the designers. For this reason, and to cover the possibility of corruption though hardware defects, the FCCs had to execute a sum check or cyclic check of the installed software. The actual type of check was considered by MAv in the light of the overall system integrity requirements as what might be considered the normal methods of checking were found to have shortcomings in that the probability objectives could not be met. This led to the introduction of more sophisticated methods to achieve the test objective. In the case of a sum check sequence to check the program and constant stores, a straightforward analysis of the probability of bit corruption in a 16K, 16 bit PROM store showed that there was a probability greater than 1 in 10^7 of a successful sum check with 2 or more bits corrupted. This led to the introduction of cyclic redundancy check methods and a probability error of less than 2.3×10^{-10}.

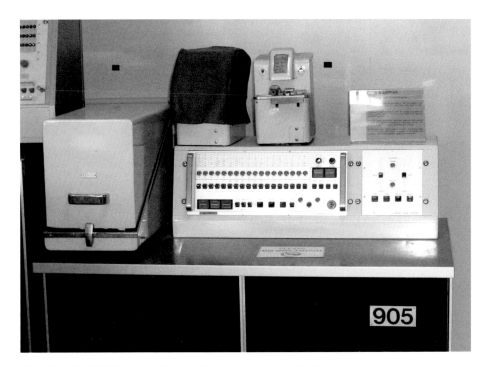

Figure 26 An Elliott 905 Computer (National Museum of Computing) (Author)

3.15.1 Software Control Procedures

MAv coded the FBW software in accordance with the BAe defined control laws and other functions. Following this process and initial testing at MAv, the software was delivered to BAe in the form of two copies of a punched paper tape, stamped with a MAv Quality Assurance mark, to indicate that the tapes were true copies of the original, kept at Rochester. The paper tapes were then used to program the FCC Programmable Read Only Memories (PROMs), care being taken to ensure that a single fault, for example a defective PROM programmer or damaged paper tape, could not result in incorrectly programmed devices. In general, testing of a new issue of software took place initially on 'A' model FCCs, with EPROM storage, prior to formal testing on 'B' model FCCs, with PROM storage. The reason for this is that during the initial stages of testing the probability of a coding problem or a changed software requirement is much higher. The rig testing of the software was in accordance with a formal set of Test Procedures.

Any problems found during the testing resulted in a Query being raised. This was a document which required a formal answer before the software could be cleared to fly. The answer could result in a change being necessary to the software, or in a change to the Test Procedure. If a change to the software was necessary, the modification to correct it may have been defined by patching the software on site at BAe, however, a new assembly and reissue of paper tapes was necessary before any formal tests could continue. If a change to the software requirement was made by BAe, this was covered on a Change Request form, signed by the appropriate authority, which was then submitted to MAv. Once formal testing was commenced on 'B' model FCCs containing the software under test, any failure to meet the requirements was assessed and appropriate corrective action taken. Any change required was classified as 'Major' or 'Minor'. A minor change was one that did not cross segregation boundaries and was contained within a small number of modules. In this event, the formal tests could continue, following receipt of the relevant program tapes from MAv. Any areas requiring retest had to be formally defined. The procedure for a minor change was successfully used for the clearance of Issue 2.8 and Issue 4.6 software. A major change (in other words anything other than a minor change) required a complete retest of the modified software. Following successful completion of the testing of an issue of software, a compliance document was raised to state that the relevant procedures had been correctly followed, and stating that the software was considered safe to fly.

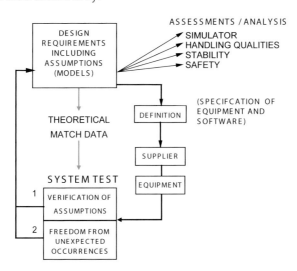

1) To verify design assumptions used and defined by control law and system designers

2) Provide assurance of no unexpected occurrences.

Figure 27 Safety Proving Process

3.15.2 Software Implementation and Safety Proving

The software requirements were defined by the System Specification and the Control Law Requirements documents, which were written by BAe. These were interpreted by MAv to generate the Software Requirements Document (SRD) and the Software Structure Document (SSD). In turn, the SRD was interpreted to produce a series of Module Design Specifications. These included the requirements of a module as a series of

FORTRAN statements, which were then hand coded into the assembler statements used by the FBW processor. The design specifications listed the various inputs and outputs of each module, the iteration rates and frame dependence, linkage details etc. A modular structure was used to break up the complex function of the software into a collection of simple functions. This provided:

• Visibility

• Ease of configuration control

• Flexibility for modification

• Ease of testing during program writing

• Eased software failure analysis

The SRD broke the software requirements down into functional areas, and into module requirements. Each module had a Design Specification and a Test Specification, the latter written by an independent programmer. The tests called up were to check that the accuracy of calculations in the module was adequate and that its requirements, as defined by the SRD, were met. The logic of the module was checked against its flow chart. Gain, limit and filter schedules were tested. The modules were assembled into their frames, and the worst-case runtimes were calculated, to ensure that the hardware defined maximum frame length could not be exceeded.

3.15.3 Software Verification

It must be remembered that at the time the software for the FBW Jaguar was being developed, there was very little experience in the qualification of safety critical software and that in academic circles there was some scepticism as to whether this could be done at all. The only projects that could provide guidance were Apollo and Concorde. From the latter came the idea of an independent audit based on a model (or emulation) developed to run on a conventional mainframe computer. At Bristol this had been an IBM360 and at Warton a slightly more up-to-date 370 was available. The task for Maths Services was to write an emulation of the aircraft processor with sufficient accuracy to run the actual flight code. This was done by Steve Brown. This turned out to be a very complex task and gave rise to many difficulties as he struggled to understand the flight computer and its software. Ultimately the process was successful and fulfilled an objective of having an independent check within the safety audit trail.

The emulation program was designed to take the machine code instructions of the target computer as data and then execute them in a representative manner. This gave a quite precise simulation of the real hardware, or rather of the way the real hardware was designed to work, although it was somewhat time consuming. The advantage was thought to be that it would gain all the facilities and back-up of a large computer and might be available before the real hardware.

In practice, to run the emulator required input signals (which in the real world come from the pilots control column and elsewhere) and in the emulation these were provided from punched cards or by another program running alongside the emulator. Similarly, the output signals (which would normally go to the control surface actuators) can be routed either to the line printer or again to another program. For an aircraft flight control computer the second program solves the aircraft differential equations of motion, thus enabling simulation of aircraft behaviour in actual flight condition. The data so obtained can then be compared with a FORTRAN description of the flight control laws and any disparities noted.

Overall, this procedure checks these points:

• Overflow within the fixed point flight processor

• Verify that all program paths are exercised (by means of a trace showing which instructions have been executed)

• Identify problems resulting from the restricted word length of the flight computer

• Check that the data store is used correctly (e.g. trying to write data in the constants area)

Eventually an excellent emulation was achieved and some real problems exposed; however, when EAP was designed, this technique was not used, as it was felt to be too expensive in relation to what was achieved.

An additional verification technique, pioneered by the BAe FCS team, involved trying to ensure that the various parts of the program, which were many low level modules, would actually come together as a whole. Given that the production process involved the breakdown of the task into low level modules, even if individually the modules might be tested as correct, it was still necessary to ensure that, when assembled, these parts would perform the intended overall task. In other words, the assembled modules must:

• Run in the correct order

• Have compatible scaling

• Be ordered to take sensor data at the appropriate time - this applies vigorously to systems using direct memory access (DMA)

For large cyclic tasks, such as flight control, groups of modules are made up into frames having an approximately equal running time. This operating pattern, whilst fairly common in real time systems, imposes the need for further care in the ordering of tasks. It is essential that data required by one processing task be calculated in a previous frame; equally it is important for control tasks that the overall data staleness, or transport delay, be minimised.

As an aid to this process, it was decided to construct a set of signal flow diagrams. These showed the running order of modules within a frame and the signals input to and output from each module. An example of such a diagram is shown below:

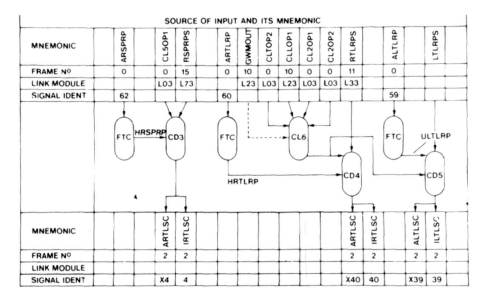

Figure 28 Signal Flow and Activity Diagram

The source of each signal was identified as either another module or direct memory access input and the signal labelled with its mnemonic. These diagrams quickly revealed inconsistencies in module order by a quick eyeball inspection, though again it was rather tedious and time consuming. Equally clearly, it was a process that could usefully have been automated. This technique was described by the author in a paper presented to the Defence Quality Assurance Board in 1980[xviii]. When first tried by the team at Warton, quite a few faults were discovered and reported to Rochester. Later, MAv used similar methods to analyse their software at Rochester.

Because of the criticality of the Jaguar's software, other MoD specialists were consulted and helped by carrying out further reviews of the software. In particular, the Royal Signals and Radar Establishment (RSRE) had a team investigating the problem of certifying safety critical software more generally. They had developed a tool called MALPASS to help with this task and submitted the software code received from Rochester to their process. They rated the software as good but not outstanding at review meetings, and made some constructive suggestions for its improvement.

At the time of the Jaguar project, other people were trying to develop tools for the better definition of software requirements. BAe at Warton had a team developing a tool called SAFRA (Semi Automated Requirements Analysis). One of the FBW team's engineers was employed in trying to convert the Jaguar's software requirements into SAFRA code. Execution of this process generated a pile of computer print out a couple of inches thick; however, it was found to be of no practical use. What was realised was that for the FCS, the bulk of the requirements were the control laws, which by definition are mathematical statements, which lend themselves to definition in software without further intervention. This led to an extremely efficient way of working when EAP was being designed; all the control laws were defined using a limited sub-set of FORTRAN instructions which were kept in a configuration controlled data base. The advantage of this way of working was that the same software could be used with the aerodynamic design programs, thus avoiding any additional translation exercises with the inevitable risk of errors.

3.15.4 Software Development

Given the somewhat limited facilities available initially at Rochester, it will perhaps be no surprise that software production was fraught with difficulties. The task was under estimated and, given the need to respect the production method imposed by safe software rules, very boring for the low level programmers. In addition, at first, MAv wanted to get all the modules written before starting testing, which then led to much re-work when faults were found. Some of the software modules were subcontracted, but the quality was poor. BAe was also volunteered by Dave Parry to write some software, but the engineers concerned, having discovered the level of boredom, threatened to leave if more was imposed. Because of all the problems, much time was taken at the regular progress meetings trying to find out just what was going on and trying to push MAv to do better. Eventually, MAv decided that the best way forward was to virtually start again, with better configuration control and did a good job.

These problems put a lot of strain on MAv's original project manager, Howard Pearce, with the result that he decided to leave the programme. He was replaced by Bob Marshall who saw the programme though to a successful conclusion. Credit is also due to Murray Gibson who led the software team and eventually got things under control, though not without at times becoming a little overexcited when the going was tough. Ian Darbyshire related how on one occasion he was rung up by Mike Tomsett (Quality Assurance Manager, Rochester), who said that he had a Scotsman going berserk in his office!

In spite of the pain of software production for the FBW Jaguar, much was learnt on both sides and when EAP started in earnest in 1984, the whole process of control law definition and software production was very much streamlined and worked extremely well. Many lessons had been learnt by all concerned.

3.16   Control Law Design

Prior to the start of design of the control laws i.e. the mathematical relationship between pilot's controls and flight control surfaces, it was necessary to have a mathematical model (aerodynamic data set) of the aircraft itself. An advantage of using the Jaguar was that models already existed of the basic aircraft, and a model suitable for control law design was made available to the team in 1976. A version for the straked, unstable aircraft, followed in 1977. A number of difficulties in the use and interpretation of these data led to the formation of a Jaguar FBW Master Data File (MDF), with the objective of providing a formal, configuration controlled computer based data set to provide consistency and integrity for all data used in theoretical calculations. This became the only source of formally accepted Jaguar FBW design data. The contents of this file were formally validated and controlled by the FBW Group, and changes to the computer store could only be made with the appropriate authorisation.

Passing this designated set of control laws to the flight simulation department allowed pilot-in-the loop assessments to be made. Pilot comment was then fed back into the design, and a fully designed set of control laws specified. Early in the programme, the simulation exercises were of limited value, as the simulator cockpit was unrepresentative of a real Jaguar. Simulation activity was later moved to the systems rig with a representative cockpit, and proceeded with the close co-operation of the FCS and flight simulation engineers and the pilots. The simulation exercises generally took the form of flight sorties similar to the flight evaluation process, unless specific design assessments were required. Occasionally, it was found necessary to 'calibrate' the pilots, by simulating a standard production Jaguar (with which the pilots were familiar), and then assessing specific areas of criticism of the Jaguar FBW system. It was found in this way that the simulator effects could be better appreciated, and criticisms became ameliorated when the general improvement on the standard Jaguar characteristics could be fully appreciated.

The design of the control laws proved to be rather more difficult than originally anticipated. First of all the team was under considerable pressure to send the laws, when they were still at an early stage and immature to MAv for software design and coding to meet the original time-scales. In addition, the designers were inexperienced and new to the design of laws to be implemented in a digital computer. A further unknown at the start of the programme was just what would constitute good handling for a pilot. This latter point led to pilot comment that an early version of the control laws had turned the Jaguar from a fighter into an airliner. Getting round these problems was a very considerable achievement and led to one of the specialists, namely John Gibson becoming a world renowned expert on handling qualities[15].

The design aim of the control laws was to give the FBW Jaguar handling qualities at least as good as the standard Jaguar over the full flight envelope and in a wide variety of configurations. The FCS also had to provide an integral stall departure and spin prevention system (SDSP) as well as to respect those load limits that are not restricted by flight limitations - for example maximum fin loads. Overall, two sets of control laws were used; one for the stable and one for the unstable pitch configurations. Both sets of laws could have been stored in the FCC, but for safety reasons were loaded separately into the computers according to the actual aircraft configuration.

---

[15] In 1991, he was awarded the Royal Aeronautical Society's Bronze Medal for innovation in handling qualities analysis and design methods. This followed his paper 'Evaluation of Alternate Handling Qualities Criteria in Highly Augmented Unstable Aircraft', AIAA-90-2844-CP, 1990.

3.16.1 Longitudinal Laws

The longitudinal control laws were based on a pitch rate plus incidence demand system. The pilot's control input was converted to a pitch rate demand and the incidence into equivalent pitch rate before being compared with pitch rate feedback. The pitch rate error signal was converted to a tailplane demand signal via a proportional, integral and differential (PID) controller. This type of controller was intended to minimise the spread (or variation) in stick force per g with aircraft configuration and manoeuvre margin and ensure good handling qualities. Pitch axis gains were scheduled with airspeed, altitude, incidence and undercarriage position. A non-linear 'manoeuvre boost' path was also included as an additional forward path in the pitch loop. This gave a marked improvement in short term response to stick inputs by combining good tracking ability with rapid response in large perturbation manoeuvres. The incidence limiting function of the SDSP was then an integral part of the longitudinal control laws.

3.16.2 Lateral Laws

The lateral control loop was a roll rate command system, wherein roll rate demand from the lateral stick was compared with actual roll rate to produce a roll rate error signal that was used to command spoiler and differential tailplane deflection. A feed forward path was included to provide good roll acceleration and the control demand necessary to maintain the desired roll rate in a steady roll. At low incidence (particularly at high speed), roll control was basically provided by the spoilers. As incidence increased (at low speed) this was augmented by differential tailplane. Thus roll control was a function of airspeed and incidence. Rudder compensation was also scheduled as a function of incidence. These interconnects between axes provided good co-ordination and roll performance and the SDSP functions were inherent in the control law scheduling.

3.16.3 Directional Laws

The directional control laws consisted of a wind axis yaw damper with sideslip feedback to augment directional stiffness. The wind axis yaw rate was synthesised from body axis yaw and roll rates. Turn entry and exit at low speed was improved using a synthesised bank angle term from a further roll rate to rudder cross-feed. Sideslip feedback was used to augment directional stability at high incidence and was available for augmentation at low incidence for low directional stability external store configurations (e.g. underwing fuel tanks). As in the roll axis, the SDSP function was inherent in the gain scheduling, for example rudder pedal authority (with undercarriage up) was progressively reduced as incidence increased in order to prevent pilot induced departures.

3.16.4 Fixed Gains and Training Mode

In the event of a double failure of the triplex secondary sensors, (i.e. incidence, sideslip, airspeed or altitude) the control laws were switched to a fixed gain mode. In this condition, all scheduling functions had to be set to fixed values and undercarriage position (from the cockpit selector switch) was used to select appropriate gains for normal flight or landing. In order to allow pilot assessment of this condition, a training mode was provided in the control laws. This was equivalent to the fixed gains mode and the pilot could select and deselect this mode via a cockpit switch marked 'Spin Recovery Mode'. The spin recovery mode was only intended for recovery from developed spins where the rate feedback terms in the normal control modes would apply adverse control inputs and hinder recovery. The spin recovery mode provided a direct position control of mean and differential tailplane, rudder and spoilers with no other motion feedback. The mode was really only a test facility for emergency use when proving the SDSP system and strictly was not therefore an integral part of the normal control laws.

3.16.5 Development

During the course of the programme, there were a number of versions or issues of the control laws. These were necessary primarily in the early phases as development proceeded and later to correspond to the various flight phases. Special editions were also written to cover, for example, spin recovery. Once the control laws were developed to a satisfactory level, they were 'frozen' ready for coding by MAv and defined in a key report kept under configuration control[xix].

4   INSTALLATION

From the above description of the system, it will be gathered that a good deal of equipment had to be installed in the Jaguar, and even though the removal of existing FCS equipment provided some room, other standard aircraft equipment had to be removed to provide space. Primarily these comprised the ammunition boxes (to provide space for the computers) and the guns (ADMCs and batteries).

Special precautions were taken to prevent electrical interference affecting the FBW equipment. This included both ordinary radio interference and the consequences of the aircraft being struck by lightning. All the main cable runs were double screened. Bonding was improved around access bay doors to maintain electrical continuity between skin and door, the aim being to achieve a Faraday cage for internal equipment. In the standard aircraft cockpit, the forward coaming consists of a composite plastic panel. This was deemed unsuitable for a FBW aircraft and so it was replaced by one of metal to provide better EMI protection.

The location of the primary components is shown in the following figure:

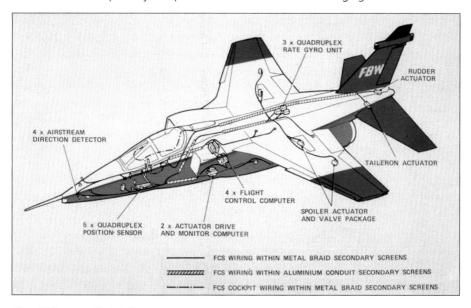

Figure 29 Equipment Installation

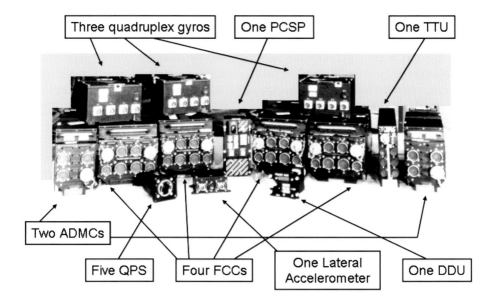

Figure 30 FBW Aircraft Equipment

The main installation problems were associated with the FCCs. As noted above these were located in what had been the ammunition boxes across the aircraft and space was fairly tight. This also meant that the connectors had to be on the front of the computers and accommodating them together with the extra cable screens was not easy. A further difficulty was caused by inexperience on the part of the engineer at Rochester tasked with sorting out the wiring schedule. At first in some cases, wires going into a single lead emerged from different connectors on the computer. The worst of these were sorted out after the design review, but even then the layout was not optimum. Basically when trying to sort out the wiring schedule it is essential to have a diagram of the connector to see which pins are adjacent, this had not been done – definitely a lesson to be learnt by MAv.

Another annoyance was found in the connectors used for the Quadruplex Position Sensors (QPS). These were standard small aircraft connectors, but it was found that those used on the QPS end were in some cases right at the small end of the physical size specification whilst the free plugs on the aircraft cables were at the maximum size limit. The result was that they were a loose fit, which was deemed unacceptable under likely condition of aircraft vibration (i.e. they might drop off). This problem was solved by wire locking the plugs to the QPS sockets.

5   QUALIFICATION

As noted under the programme objectives, a main aim of the programme was the qualification of the system for flight. Therefore, both prior to starting and throughout the programme considerable effort was devoted to this topic. Although the main problem area was perceived as being the software, every aspect had to be considered and many points gave rise to much head scratching. In retrospect, the necessary approach appears obvious and indeed many of the necessary procedures were appreciated at the time. What was not clear was how all the parts should be drawn together. Some parts of the process were very similar to those for existing aircraft, others entirely new.

Thus in the case of the computers, for example, the environmental qualification could follow established practice in terms of vibration, temperature altitude etc. Electromagnetic compatibility (EMC) testing also followed existing military specifications, but it was recognised that these were really of limited value in that they were considered not to be sufficiently demanding for FBW aircraft. For this reason the Jaguar was used extensively to further develop EMC test methods after the conclusion of its flying programme.

The process of qualification may be stated very simply: does the equipment function as intended, and is it free from unwanted characteristics? Documentary evidence is necessary to support this contention and if care is not exercised, its bulk may overwhelm those concerned. Thus at the start of any new programme the objectives of the clearance process need to be clearly laid out through a 'route to qualification'; difficult when carrying it out for the first time. What was recognised was that a system has to be designed with safety and qualification in mind from the start - it certainly cannot be added-on later - and so meetings were held early in the programme with the Airworthiness and Reliability departments.

As an example of the problems that can arise, initially MAv Rochester sub-contracted the Failure Modes and Effects Analysis (FMEA) to another branch of GEC. This proved far from satisfactory, but in addition, the manner in which faults were classified, as originally specified by BAe, was not too good either. This led to a re-definition of FMEA codes and these were used in mildly modified form for later projects.

5.1   Testing the System

5.1.1   Ground Test Rig

The Jaguar FBW ground test rig existed to explore all aspects of the flight control system (FCS) performance and to ensure that the system met the design requirements. The main components of the rig comprised:

• Flight Control Computer (FCC) benches. Two full benches were provided to facilitate parallel testing

- Sensor bench, designed for testing of the incidence, sideslip and air data transducers
- Actuator benches comprising representative actuator mounting structures with facilities for applying loads
- A three-axis rate table
- A representative cockpit containing pilot's controls, instruments and a computer generated outside world display
- A flight simulation computer
- A Data Acquisition and Simulation/Stimulation System (DASS)

The various components of the rig could be used in isolation to test individual items of equipment, or together, whereby a pilot could 'fly' the complete FCS fully closed loop. In addition, the cockpit and simulation computer could be used to assess and develop the different standards of control laws required during the programme.

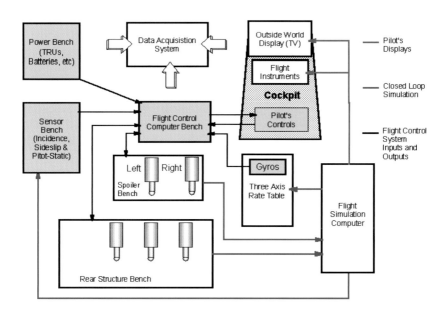

Figure 31 The Rig System

Building the rig was a large task in its own right that took a couple of years. It was decided that the rig would be housed in a new building that would form an extension to 7 Hangar. This was very convenient as the main engineering team was housed in the office space of the System Development Department, also in 7 Hangar, whilst the aircraft conversion was carried out at the airfield end of the same building. This co-location of

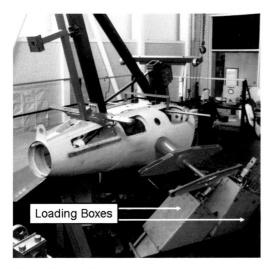

Figure 32 Rig Rear Structure

many members of the different disciplines working on the project engendered a very good team spirit and motivation as everyone could see what was happening and how their effort fitted into the whole project.

Comprehensive facilities were provided to house the actuators on representative structures including the rear end of a scrap Jaguar for the taileron actuators. Also visible in figure 32 are the loading boxes (springs) for actuator testing. The loading boxes were actually recovered from an English Electric Lightning rig.

The spoilers demanded their own test bench, which was built from scratch. The spoilers also differed from the other actuators in that because of limited space for installation, the valve block had to be mounted remotely from the actuator main ram cylinders. This arrangement and layout was correctly represented on the rig.

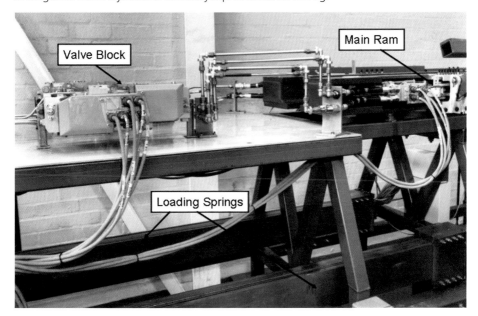

Figure 33 Spoiler bench

The computer benches accommodated the four FCCs and two ADMCs. The earliest deliveries of equipment (the 'A' models) comprised computers in six-foot racks that stood alongside the rig benches. The later aircraft units had to be provided with cooling air and hence sat on plenum chambers equipped with fans.

Figure 34 Computer Bench and Three-Axis Rate Table

Figure 35 The Rig and Cockpit

Figure 36 The Rig Cockpit and Outside World Display

For pilot in the loop testing, a fixed base cockpit was provided on the rig linked to a Digital Equipment Corporation (DEC) PDP 11 simulation computer. Within the cockpit, a full set of flying controls (using actual aircraft parts) was combined with head up display and outside world display. Other essential flying instruments (e.g. airspeed, altitude) were fitted and driven by the simulation computer. Other parts were simplified to white on black prints of the missing instruments. As an example, the moving map display can be seen in the photo located above the stick.

The Data Acquisition and Simulation/Stimulation System (DASS) was designed and built by BAe's in-house Electronics Department at Warton. The DASS comprised three main subsystems:

• The simulation computer and outside world display. This used a PDP 11 computer to provide simulation of the aircraft aerodynamics (flight mechanics) and a simulation of the standard Jaguar for comparison with the FBW aircraft. The output of this computer drove the cockpit flight instruments together with a fairly basic outside world display. For closed loop testing it could take flight control surface position and additionally output data representing aircraft rates and air data to feed into the FCCs. Options were provided to either drive the sensors themselves (e.g. gyros via the three axis rate table) or directly into the FCCs. The latter option was used for the majority of testing because of the sluggish behaviour of the rate table. Inevitably lag between the simulation computer and the large rate table meant that it was not really practical for closed loop testing. The inner gimbal was lighter and electrically driven (the outer being hydraulic) and so was fast enough for some tests. This was a project 'lesson learnt' and a full rate table was not used on EAP

• The main data acquisition computer, again a PDP 11, took incoming information from the rig for display and recording. It could also run some automated tests, but this was not its primary purpose

• The Continuous Recording Facility. This contrivance allowed the data on the computer-computer data links out of each FCC to be continuously recorded. Under normal conditions a total of about seven seconds recording time was available covering the outputs of all four FCCs. This limitation was very much a reflection of then existing computer hardware; even this needed a twelve-inch hard drive and dedicated PDP 11 computer. In practice it was normally set up to continuously overwrite data until a trigger, such as a detected failure, occurred. This generally resulted in the storage of five seconds of data preceding the event and two seconds after it

5.1.2   Rig Testing

Rig testing absorbed several years of effort prior to the first flight. The objective of this activity is sometimes misunderstood because the first object is to assemble equipment and 'get it working', and for the uninitiated, this appears to be the end of the matter. For safety critical systems there is much more because of the need to demonstrate that it meets the safety objectives. However, testing as such cannot prove that a system meets the 'reliability' requirements; such evidence can only come from a fleet of aircraft over their lifetime (e.g. hundreds of thousands of operating hours), and so a plan is necessary to show that the system is safe in a reasonable time. The task must therefore be broken down into segments that can be achieved in a reasonable time whilst satisfying the need to demonstrate that the safety objectives have been met. The main test phases may be broken down as follows:

- To check out individual components or equipments as delivered by manufacturers. In production, this is known as acceptance testing and is generally limited to making sure that equipment is working through meeting a limited subset of the specification requirements. However, in development much more testing may be needed to fully develop and qualify components

- The integration of the various parts into subsystems, and then the integration of these into the complete flight control system

- To verify design assumptions; these arise because the design process makes assumptions as to how the system should work (e.g. through computer models) and these may or may not be correct

- Provide assurance of no unexpected occurrences

The second of these activities is generally described as informal testing, even though much of the testing will be to defined test procedures. This is because the object is to understand and get the system working. Now since it does not form part of the flight clearance, the correction of faults and changes to software are relatively easy in terms of documentation.

Formal testing is carried out on a configuration-controlled set of hardware and software. This means that any changes have to be justified and tracked by Quality Assurance in a formal manner to a set procedure. The overall process may be summarised in the following figure:

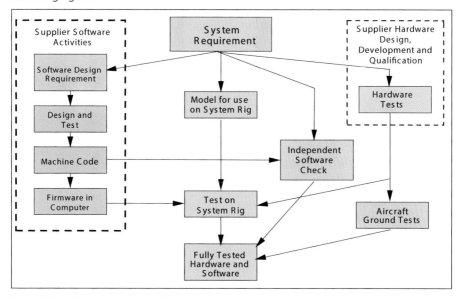

Figure 37 Test Concept and Route to Clearance

It may be wondered why development testing takes so long, but with complex systems it may not be obvious where a problem lies. At one point in rig testing strange things appeared to be happening in that although the system appeared to be working normally, the Continuous Recording Facility (CRF) appeared to indicate that the FCCs were sometimes missing software frames. Under these conditions, there were two possible causes, either the FCCs really were missing frames or the CRF was failing to record them. Arguments went on for some months with both sides (MAv for the FCC and Warton's Electronics Department for the CRF) insisting that they were right and that their equipment could not possibly be wrong. Eventually, the author devised a test to resolve matters; the fault was in the priority arbitration logic of the CRF.

5.1.3   An Extra Test

Although the above process, in conjunction with the rig described above appeared at the start of the rig test programme to be sufficient, the engineering manager (Dave Parry) was not fully satisfied. It will be seen from the rig system diagram that for closed loop tests a digital FCS was complemented by a digital representation of the aircraft aerodynamics (flight mechanics) run on a simulation computer. Therefore, the accuracy of the representation depended on yet more assumptions and approximations. It was decided to design and build a simple analogue computer for comparison with the digital simulation.

Dave Parry derived the equations of motion and the author designed the computer. It was only capable of single flight conditions (fixed speed and height) but did provide additional assurance that nothing had slipped through the net. It was also a nice demonstration of the benefit of having managers who really understand in detail the characteristics of the system they are managing. Today this is much more rarely the case, a manager with a degree in Business Administration is thought to be capable of managing anything, but when problems arise may not have the experience to know what is relevant.

5.2   Aircraft Ground Test Equipment

A mobile semi-automated test set (trolley) was provided for first-line on-aircraft testing of the digital FCS and associated sensors. This equipment was very similar to the rig DASS, but designed for transportability. It was based on another DEC computer, the PDP 11-33, and had three good quality colour monitors for the display of information together with a printer and chart recorder. The trolley included storage for a reasonable length of cable to connect to the FCC test connectors. This equipment proved invaluable for carrying out many forms of testing, including:

• General system check out

• Structural coupling tests

• Ground testing with and without engines running

• Warton airfield EMC testing

- EMC testing at Aircraft and Armament Experiment Establishment, Boscombe Down
- Simulated lightning strike testing at Warton

As with the DASS, it was designed and built by the Electronics Department at Warton. Because of its size, it was constructed in a wooden hut adjacent to the Electronics main building. At the end of this process, a wall was demolished to get the trolley out of the hut!

Figure 38 Aircraft Ground Test Equipment (EMC Testing at Boscombe Down)

5.3   Lightning Testing

Lightning can pose a threat to conventional aircraft with basic mechanical controls and was seen early on as being a very significant risk to a FBW aircraft. Meetings were therefore arranged with experts in the field at RAE Farnborough and more especially with the Culham Lightning Studies Unit, Abingdon during 1978. Initial discussions were concerned with educating BAe personnel with the nature and magnitude of lightning strikes, and basic measures needed to protect the aircraft and its systems. In addition, Culham mentioned that they could develop a portable lightning current generator suitable for testing the Jaguar at levels representative of a real lightning strike[xx].

Plans for lightning strike testing were further developed over the next couple of years so that a properly costed proposal could be submitted to the MoD as this work had not been part of the original FBW contract. In November 1981, a meeting was arranged for the RAE and Culham experts to inspect the aircraft and provide comments and advice. At this stage they were quite critical of some aspects of the installation[xxi] and whilst some points could be dealt with fairly easily, others really had to await the next aircraft (EAP).

Simulated lightning strike tests were arranged to take place in the break after the first phase of test flying. Until these tests had taken place the aircraft was under a severe restriction that it must not fly if lightning were at all likely. Testing took place during 1982 after permission had been received from BAe's fire and aviation insurers. A portable generator was brought to Warton and located with the aircraft and other test equipment in 7 Hangar. Test currents were injected into the nose and then taken back from the tail via a set of return conductors arranged around the fuselage (to minimise loop inductance). Maximum currents up to 80,000 Ampères could be injected, representing about a quarter of a real lightning strike. Dummy computers equipped with instrumentation were used to measure the voltages induced into aircraft wiring. These were coupled to a screened instrumentation room by means of fibre optic cables. Specialists from the RAE Farnborough also participated in the tests – they were interested in measuring the bulk currents induced into the cables as the basis of tests to be used on future aircraft[xxii].

In general, the FCS coped extremely well with this abuse, but some improvements were made to cable screening, particularly around the cockpit - an area that was always anticipated as being especially vulnerable. One piece of standard aircraft was destroyed in the course of the tests, an aerial on top of the fin 'popped' when the return currents were taken from the fin top.

The Jaguar FBW lightning tests clearly indicated that a continuous metal airframe is the best protection against lightning, the implication being that future aircraft, with composite construction, would need very careful design if problems were to be avoided.

Figure 39 Lightning Test Rig

5.4   Spin Recovery Facilities

Special arrangements had to be made to ensure safety during all high incidence testing carried out on the aircraft. These measures were basically similar to those used during standard Jaguar spinning trials, namely additional instruments, in-flight telemetry, a spin recovery parachute and canopy fragilisation system. The canopy fragilisation system, which consisted of a miniature detonating cord attached to the canopy, was fitted throughout the flight trials of the FBW Jaguar, whereas on the standard Jaguar it was only fitted for high incidence trials.

Changes to the cockpit for high incidence testing included a white warning light activated below 25,000 ft. or -2 g longitudinal acceleration (indicating that the spin recovery chute should be deployed), an audio eject warning activated at 10,000 ft., spin recovery parachute controls, and incidence and sideslip gauges covering a range much greater than the standard instruments. These were fitted in a prominent position above the coaming to the left of the Head Up Display (HUD). The spin recovery parachute replaced the normal, larger diameter brake parachute, and was a developed version of the equipment previously used on Jaguar. The parachute would be deployed by means of a steel 'bullet' and drogue parachute, and could be released at any flight attitude using an explosive jettison device. The normal brake parachute was fitted for all other flying.

5.5   Flight Test Instrumentation

The Flight Test Instrumentation (FTI) system is shown below. The main system was based on a programmable data acquisition system (pDAS) manufactured by Base Ten Systems and a 14-track magnetic tape recorder (MARS 2000) manufactured by Bell and Howell. This provided the capability to record up to ten channels of analogue data and one channel of digital (PCM) data, cockpit voice, time-code and a reference frequency (to monitor tape speed). All digital data was processed by the pDAS, which converted digital and analogue inputs into a PCM stream with defined sampling rates and frame structure. Digital data was supplied to the pDAS by a small number of digital (frequency) transducers and, through a specially designed interface unit, by FCC 4. The digital stream supplied by the FCC included a window of 6 words multiplexed to provide up to 48 parameters to the instrumentation system. This window could be programmed to include any word in the memory of FCC 4, which might also include words supplied across lane from the other FCC's.

The pDAS was supplied with analogue data via a patch-board, transducers and signal conditioners being fitted as necessary to measure standard aircraft parameters. Data was also supplied in analogue form by FCC 4, a range of analogue outputs being available at the computer's test connector in addition to the digital stream. Data to be recorded in analogue form was routed to the recorder via the group selector box instead of the pDAS. Any one of up to four groups of 10 parameters could be recorded at a given time, group selection being by pilot switch. Analogue inputs were provided by individual transducers / signal conditioners and by the FCC 4 analogue outputs.

The in-flight telemetry and accident data recorder systems were as used on development Jaguars, and as such independent of the main instrumentation system. For telemetry a conventional FM/FM, 14 channel analogue system was used together with existing Jaguar ground station equipment. The accident recorder was a Sperry wire type capable of recording 46 data samples per second. Both these systems had dedicated transducers and signal conditioning independent of the FCS.

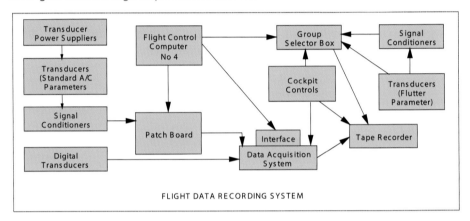

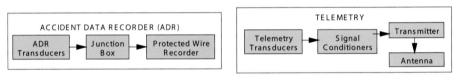

Figure 40 On-Aircraft Data Recording and Telemetry

Normal Jaguar equipment and procedures were employed in the telemetry ground station, which even by the standards of the time (e.g. the Tornado ground station) was fairly basic.

6   FLIGHT TRIALS

A detailed flight test programme was prepared for the original proposal and then progressively updated in the light of experience. There were three main parts: initial flight trials with fixed gain control laws to develop confidence in the equipment and aircraft systems, fully scheduled control laws (to provide better handling) leading to carefree manoeuvring and finally demonstration of the control of an aerodynamically unstable vehicle. Two pilots shared the bulk of test flying, namely Chris Yeo and Pete Orme. The flight test programme was spread over three years from the first flight in 1981 until the end of the project in 1984[xxiii].

6.1   First Flight

Figure 41 First Flight take-off

Chris Yeo took the aircraft up for its first flight on October 20th 1981. The flight went very well, especially considering the novelty of the system. He can be seen (in the following picture) looking absolutely delighted, alongside Ollie Heath, the engineering director.

Figure 42 Post First Flight – Chris Yeo and Ollie Heath, Engineering Director

At essentially the same time, photographs were also taken of some of the personnel involved in the programme to celebrate a successful first flight.

Figure 43 The Team - 1. Left to right: JR Nelson, E Daley, C Yeo, B Phillipson, MD Parry, WA Boardman, D Allison, P Culbert, BRC Weller, DS Nicoll, IT Darbyshire, AP Greco, P Wood

Figure 44 The Team - 2. Left to right: DE Corner, J Taylor, D Edmunson, RG Calvert, SG Burns, TL Wain, AJ Agnew, JD Baggaley, A Bousfield, SP Crompton, D Gasser

6.2   Initial Trials - Phases (a) and (b)

The objectives of Phase (a) of the flight trials comprised a basic shakedown of the airframe, engines and standard aircraft systems; preliminary assessment of the flight control system; confirmation of safe aircraft handling within a limited flight envelope and checks of air data sensor calibration. These trials led straight into Phase (b) of the trials which had the additional objectives of flutter testing to clear the full flight envelope, and a more detailed handling assessment to include rapid rolling and ground attack dives, as well as testing up to 'trials only' limitations. These two phases were to be performed using Issue 1A control laws in the fixed gain (Training) mode.

The flight trials commenced in October 1981, and Phase (a) flying was completed in five flights compared with the planned six to ten flights. Phase (b) flying commenced on November 19th 1981. It proved so successful that it was completed in eight flights, compared with the programmed eight to twelve flights. Aircraft handling was assessed up to 550 knots / 1.26 Mach, and the aircraft proved to be very easy to fly, with no sign of pilot induced oscillation (PIO) or over-control, and the characteristics were in general as good as, if not better than the standard Jaguar. In addition, the general handling assessment, rapid rolling, formation flying, aerobatics, ground attack tracking and turbulence penetration were also assessed with very satisfactory results. Two characteristics were criticised in the course of the handling assessment, a 'roll hunting' phenomenon at high subsonic speeds and poor handling in Spin Recovery Mode.

Roll hunting (also known as 'threepenny bit rolling') was found to be due to poor damping of the roll stick; in the standard Jaguar there is enough friction in the control linkage but this was of course absent on the FBW Jaguar. A hydraulic damper was therefore added, and later flying demonstrated that this completely cured the problem. Poor handling in Spin Recovery Mode was analysed and once understood resulted in modifications to the next issue of flight software.

The flutter test programme successfully cleared the aircraft to 600 knots at high altitude, and 550 knots below 20,000 ft, but initially with a low altitude limit of 500 knots with issue 1 software. FCS behaviour was very good, with no flights being lost or curtailed due to FCS failures. Only one FCS failure warning occurred in flight (flight 13), and this was caused by a delay in the operation of individual poles of the quadruplex undercarriage selector switch (see paragraph 3.9).

6.3   The Fully Scheduled Control Laws
- Phases (c) and (d)

The main objective of Phase (c) of the flight trials programme was a detailed assessment of Issue 2 fully scheduled control laws in normal mode throughout the clean aircraft flight envelope. This included flutter testing to clear the full flight envelope of the standard Jaguar, as well as verification of secondary sensor operation and an assessment of Training mode and Spin Recovery mode. These trials were to lead straight into Phase

(d) with the objectives of extending the Issue 2 assessment to the aircraft fitted with underwing fuel tanks, at normal and reduced levels of longitudinal stability.

The Phase (c) trials commenced on November 10th 1982. They were completed in nine flights, despite delays caused by engine problems and not by the new FCS. Phase (d) commenced on March 10th 1983, and completed in just five flights. Aircraft handling was assessed up to 625 knots / 1.25 Mach for the clean aircraft, and 580 knots / 0.95 Mach for the aircraft with underwing tanks. In both configurations, handling qualities were assessed as very good, particularly with tanks fitted. This was an area where the FBW Jaguar represented a significant improvement in handling over the standard Jaguar. A minimum manoeuvre margin[16] of +2% č was demonstrated with excellent results. The actions taken to resolve the characteristics criticised during the Issue 1A assessment were shown to be successful. In addition to the general handling assessment, rapid rolling, formation flying, air-to-air and air-to-ground tracking and turbulence response were assessed, with generally very satisfactory results. In particular, rapid rolling was assessed as excellent. The only criticisms were of the slightly harsh pitch response (manoeuvre boost nudge), the somewhat looser response in turbulence compared with Issue 1 control laws and a reverse trim effect in pitch. FCS performance continued to be generally very good. However, a small number of secondary sensor failures were encountered, the majority of which were caused by problems with air data sensors.

An additional two flights (one in each configuration) were then flown by an RAE pilot (Roger Searle). These went quite well, but it was noted that whereas the BAe pilots were already familiar with the feel of an augmented aircraft (Tornado), this was new to Roger Searle and he found it somewhat disconcerting at times. He commented that it 'felt as though there were someone else in the cockpit'.

6.4   Carefree Manoeuvring - Phase (f)

The objective of Phase (f) of the flight trials was a demonstration of the successful integration of the Stall Departure and Spin Prevention Function in the FCS control laws. As a prerequisite to the trial, a number of test deployments of the spin recovery parachute were defined as well as engine testing. Checks were devised to assess handling in Spin Recovery mode and other associated features. The test phase first started in February 1983, with ground and in flight test streams of the spin recovery parachute. However, a premature failure of the parachute weak link required a re-design of the weak link, and the trial was delayed until April 1983. The parachute testing was then successfully completed, and the high incidence trial commenced. Phase (f) was completed in 10 flights with excellent results. During the seven high incidence test flights, 43 manoeuvre sequences were performed at full back stick, and despite very aggressive manoeuvring, there were no signs of incipient departure, and the aircraft was completely under control at all times. A progressive series of tests was performed by the two pilots working up

---

[16] Manoeuvre margin is defined as the percentage of wing mean chord. The symbol generally used is a 'c' with two bars above. Limitation of the character set available led to the use of 'č' in this document.

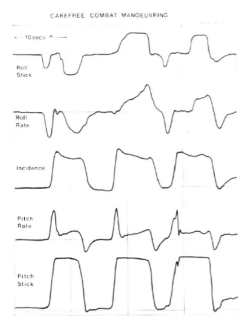

Figure 45 Carefree Manoeuvring

to very severe dynamic manoeuvres, and concluding with a simulated combat assessment by each pilot. Both pilots were very satisfied with the aircraft behaviour, and the trials results generated a very high level of pilot confidence in the SDSP system, to the extent that the FCS could be described as providing virtually 'carefree manoeuvring' within the aircraft g limits. FCS behaviour continued to be good, but one flight was curtailed by a series of SENSOR warnings.

This part of the test programme was considered as demonstrating very conclusively the advantages of FBW. On a standard Jaguar the incidence limit for normal flying is just 16°. This is necessary to give a safety margin for ordinary service pilots below the point where spin departure is likely. On the FBW Jaguar, the pilot could safely pull the stick hard back and wait for the system to sort things out and limit incidence to around 23°. It was also demonstrated that the system would deal with diagonal stick pulls – in other words the pilot could safely demand maximum roll and pitch rate simultaneously – in a standard Jaguar this would be guaranteed to result in loss of control. Figure 45 is taken from the flight test results.

6.5   Unstable Flight - Phase (e)

Phase (e[17]) of the trials defined the first assessment of a longitudinally unstable configuration. The overall objective was to demonstrate satisfactory aircraft behaviour with Issue 3 control laws, in aircraft configurations providing manoeuvre margins in the range + 3% č to -4% č. A revised tailplane flap angle was required from tailplane jack load considerations, and a prerequisite of the Issue 3 assessment was a flight with Issue 2 laws in a stable configuration, in order to measure jack loads with the new tailplane flap angle.

This test phase began on July 4th 1983, with the jack load assessment flight with Issue 2 control laws. Following a deployment to Boscombe Down for High Frequency Radio susceptibility testing during the remainder of July and early August, the first flight with

[17] Note that the various phases were defined in the original programme plan, but that (e) and (f) were later executed in the order stated here.

Issue 3 laws took place on August 15th. The test phase was completed in nine flights, of which two were in the nominal 0% č configuration (underwing tanks with auto fuel sequence), and six in the nominal -3% č manoeuvre margin configuration (underwing tanks with manual fuel sequence).

This trial was completely successful. Handling qualities were excellent in all axes throughout the envelope assessed (580 knots / 0.95 Mach), in normal mode, and a manoeuvre margin of -4% č was achieved. Rapid rolling characteristics were excellent, and the characteristics criticised during Issue 2 flying ('manoeuvre boost nudge', loose response in turbulence and a reverse trim effect), were completely absent. Training mode handling was assessed as satisfactory as a reversionary mode, being entirely adequate for its 'get you home' role.

Air-to-air and air-to-ground tracking characteristics were rated as very good, as was aircraft behaviour during formation flying, aerobatics and turbulence penetration. The fact that the aircraft was in an aerodynamically unstable configuration was undetectable by the pilot from the handling qualities, only after touchdown was the very aft centre of gravity position evident, since a firm stick forward input was required to de-rotate the aircraft. FCS performance continued to be very good apart from a number of SENSOR warnings. The conclusion was that this was due to the value of incidence derived from the two sideslip probes being too sensitive to small angular errors. However, it was recognised from the outset that the Jaguar nose is not particularly good in this respect. Despite this fact, the highly successful SDSP trial indicated that even with a 'non optimum' shape, the FCS design was tolerant enough to use these derived signals successfully in the area where they were most important.

6.6   Pilot Comment – Chris Yeo

Chris Yeo wrote an article for the March 1984 edition of the BAe in-house magazine Intercomm in which he described his experiences flying Jaguar FBW over its first two years of flight trials. It is worth recalling this period because it outlines the gradual transition from stable flight to an unstable configuration that was such an essential precursor for the design of EAP. It is also helpful to hear the words of the pilot who accepted the inevitable risks involved in developing the system.

He said (of the FBW Jaguar) '[I have] been continuously involved in testing this new kind of control system since it first flew on 20th October 1981. Since then it has flown 50 times and has generated a mass of technical data for analysis. More importantly perhaps it has given the Warton designers a great deal of confidence in their ability to put together a flight control system using modern techniques of digital computing which will be compatible with any future combat aircraft.

The FBW Jaguar began life as the 62nd production single-seat Jaguar and served with the RAF for some 330 hours before it was returned to Warton to be modified to become the FBW demonstrator. Most of the purely military equipment such as the two cannons and the laser were removed along with all of the mechanical control rods, apart from those which connect the control column and rudder pedals to the feel units. This change means that the pilot cannot move the surfaces directly, only the four digital computers can do that.

Thus, from the first and throughout every flight of this programme, the safety of the aircraft depends entirely on the correct functioning of the FBW control system and its attendant software; there is no way that the pilot can by-pass the electrical flight control system. Indeed once the aircraft has been de-stabilised in pitch as it was towards the end of the last flight programme and will be again this year, it would have been disastrous to do so, since the aircraft is beyond the ability of any human unaided by a computer, to control anyway. If your bank computer has yet again just coughed up a statement attributing the national debt to your personal account and you are saying 'this man is a fool' consider this. Unlike your bank (or mine come to that), the FBW system was designed so that no failure which could cause the loss of the aircraft would happen more often than once in 10 million flying hours. Or to put it another way, since King Alfred burned the cakes, give or take the odd year or two. All of you who drive to work take a considerably greater risk every day of your lives.

Having said all that and convinced that it was easy, it wasn't. Achieving reliability like that takes a prodigious effort. Take, for example, the computer software, the laws which tell the computer what to do. These were designed and then tested on a dedicated rig/simulator well before the aircraft ever left the ground. Inevitably the first attempts were not perfect or even all that good, but over several years and literally hundreds of hours of work, they got better and better. Even so, sometimes after weeks of work, a new fault would be uncovered, which meant going back to the drawing board to start the process again. It says a lot for those involved that their enthusiasm remained undiminished throughout this period.

However, by October 1981, the long process of design and ground testing had come to the ultimate test – the first flight. In fact, the flight control system was actually ready to go before the 20th October but the aircraft obviously was not, since it gave an unusual display of temperament, suffering two quite independent low technology failures of the rear tank fuel pumps and their wiring. Looking back, I can forgive the aircraft this little foible, since that time it has taken on the more usual Jaguar characteristic – rugged and reliable.

The 20th October dawned like any other first flight day at Warton, a cold gusting crosswind off the Irish Sea, bringing heavy rain showers across the airfield. Nevertheless, by judicious use of intervals between showers the flight was successfully completed. Right from the first, the aircraft flew well and quickly gave a feeling of confidence. Of course I was extremely busy throughout the flight carrying out the various scheduled tests, but I was able to pause after thirty minutes to reflect that for every second of flight the computers smoothly completed all the necessary calculations fifty times. After this philosophical thought pragmatism returned and the flight progresses as smoothly as before.

Of all the many characteristics of this first issue of the control laws, two stood out. First, the control forces were commendably light and pleasant and the aircraft responded smoothly and accurately to the smallest of control inputs. This made the aircraft pleasant and rewarding to fly. Secondly, in common with all FBW aircraft, the control system can differentiate between motion demanded by the pilot and that caused by turbulence. As I have said, it responded to the pilot's demands very well and turbulence was ruthlessly suppressed. This characteristic is a very desirable one in a combat aircraft which must deliver weapons accurately. The handling in the cockpit was similar to driving rapidly along a cobbled road, but without the motion which would be usual in a car.

The first thirteen flights used the first issue of the computer software. One of the benefits of digital computing is that the software can be changed as and when required. Of course, since the FBW Jaguar depends absolutely on the correct functioning of the software, it was necessary to go through a long and detailed process of proving that each new issue of software does what is expected of it, and only what is expected of it. So even while the aircraft was flying those first few flights, a new revised issue of software was approaching qualification.

The second issue of software introduced control laws which varied with height, airspeed, incidence and sideslip. Scheduling of the control laws like this is necessary to maintain the good flying characteristics already demonstrated by the first issue of software over a wider flight envelope and to allow carefree handling. The new control laws were a great success and all three of the pilots who flew the aircraft enjoyed themselves enormously, especially when the test schedule called for lots of hard manoeuvring and rapid rolling.

In normal aircraft, the pilot has to monitor incidence closely during manoeuvring flight. Failure to do this conscientiously can end, at best, in a temporary loss of control or, at worst, in a spin, neither of which is a good idea in combat or at low level. In the FBW Jaguar, the computers will not allow the aircraft to exceed a given limit. Furthermore, within this incidence limit the pilot can do what he likes with the controls. The computers will adjust his demands to the control surfaces so that the aircraft manoeuvres as rapidly as possible without leaving controlled flight. As an added bonus, the computers are quick enough to control the aircraft at a higher incidence than a human pilot. Hence the expression 'care-free handling'. The second issue of the control laws allowed us to explore fully the aircraft's behaviour. Despite some gross and aggressive manoeuvring during the eight hours last summer, the aircraft always remained totally under control and never at any time showed any tendency towards a departure from controlled flight. A truly impressive performance.

The third and final issue of software to be flown to date allowed the aircraft to be de-stabilised in pitch. This ability to control an unstable aircraft is one of the major benefits of a computerised control system. Conventional aircraft have to be stable for an unaided human pilot to control them; unfortunately, to achieve stability the tail-plane has to carry a download. Thus the wings not only have to lift the weight of the aircraft, but also have to compensate for the download on the tail-plane. Hence the wings have to be bigger than strictly necessary for any given aircraft and so does the rest of the structure. Furthermore, the natural stability of the aircraft tends to oppose manoeuvres. All of this changes if a computer, working far more quickly than a human pilot, can control an unstable aircraft while giving the pilot the impression of flying one with conventional control surfaces. Then the aircraft can be designed so that the tail-plane (or canard in the case of EAP) helps rather than hinders the overall performance. This is exactly what the third issue of the control laws did. The naturally stable Jaguar was de-stabilised by changing the fuel transfer sequence and by adding ballast in the tail (moving cg aft). In this state it flew very well and the instability was completely undetectable in flight, even to a pilot aware of the change.'

At the time that Chris wrote this, the aircraft was being fitted with two large strakes, or leading edge extensions along the air intake boxes. The intention was to move the centre of lift forward and allow the aircraft to be further de-stabilised in pitch. The new control laws for this configuration were defined and promised to give the same high standard of control as the previous issue of software. The aircraft was to fly in this state in early 1984.

6.7   The Highly Unstable Aircraft - Phases (g) and (h)

Phases (g) and (h) represented the final stage of the flight trials with the overall objective of flight assessment of highly unstable aerodynamic configurations. The aircraft was fitted with large leading edge strakes which moved the centre of lift forward by 11% č to provide the required levels of instability. Phase (g) represented the clean configurations, with Phase (h) the configurations with underwing tanks. In summary:

Clean Aircraft (g):

1)   Nominal +3% č required 75 kg forward ballast in nose.

2)   Nominal -4.5% č required 290 kg aft ballast.

With Underwing Wing Tanks (h):

1)   Nominal -2% č requiring 194 kg aft ballast.

2)   Nominal -10% č requiring 290 kg aft ballast + revised fuel sequencing.

The resulting new aerodynamic and structural modes had to be verified in flight in a safe configuration before proceeding to higher levels of pitch instability. In order to maximise the possible flight envelope, three sets of control laws were used. Four configurations were therefore flown to give a nominal test range of +3% to -10% č manoeuvre margin.

The flight trials programme for the four configurations was defined in two stages. The first (straked) configuration to be flown (configuration 14, clean aircraft with forward ballast) represented a target manoeuvre margin of + 3% č and was as flown with Issue 2 control laws. The main objectives of the flight trials in this configuration were to carry out an initial handling assessment of the straked aircraft, and to perform a series of manoeuvres to provide data for derivative extraction, in order to confirm the validity of the aerodynamic model used for the unstable configuration clearances.

The next configuration to be flown (configuration 15 - clean aircraft with aft ballast) represented a target manoeuvre margin of -4.5% č. This was to be flown with Issue 4 Mode 6 control laws. A full flight assessment was performed including rapid rolling, tracking, formation flying and turbulence penetration.

In Phase (h), the first configuration to be flown (configuration 18 - underwing tanks with forward ballast), represented a target manoeuvre margin of –2% č, and was to be flown with Issue 4 Mode 4 control laws (equivalent to Issue 3 control laws). The objectives for this configuration were similar to configuration 14, i.e. an initial handling assessment of the strakes + tanks configuration, and data extraction to verify the aerodynamic interference effects of strakes with underwing tanks.

The final configuration (configuration 19 - underwing tanks with aft ballast), represented a target manoeuvre margin of -10% č, and was to be flown with Issue 4 Mode 6 control laws. A full flight assessment was to be performed including rapid rolling, tracking, formation flying and turbulence penetration. The first flight in the strakes configuration took place on March 15th 1984, and the initial assessment was completed in four flights. An increasing number of sensor failures occurred during these flights, and in order to alleviate the situation, a sideslip probe re-alignment was defined and incorporated. An additional flight was performed to verify the re-alignment and it was completely successful. The initial handling assessment confirmed that handling qualities were as predicted, being very similar to earlier Issue 2 flying without strakes, but with a noticeable improvement in performance. Analysis of the data gathering manoeuvres confirmed that the aerodynamic data set used for flight clearances was valid.

The first flight with Issue 4 Mode 6 control laws took place on May 16th 1984 in the clean configuration, and the flight assessment of this configuration was completed in seven flights over a three-week period, with very satisfactory results. The detailed handling assessment demonstrated good handling qualities over the whole of the subsonic and supersonic envelopes flown. Rapid rolling characteristics were described as excellent, and overall pilot opinion was that the control laws standard was the best achieved on the programme. The only minor criticisms were the slight over response of the aircraft to turbulence in yaw, and to a lesser extent in roll, and the activity of the controls in the approach configuration with undercarriage up. However, both BAe pilots felt that the response to moderate to severe turbulence was commendably good. The performance improvements noted in the earlier flying with strakes were evident throughout the flying, and tracking behaviour in ground attack dives proved to be generally good. FCS behaviour was very good throughout the period.

The first flight in the strakes plus tanks configuration (Phase h) took place on June 20th, and the data gathering flight trials in configuration 18 were successfully completed in 3 flights. The trials included the first assessment of air-to-air refuelling (dry contacts against a Victor Tanker), as well as formation flying and air-to-air, and air-to-ground tracking. Analysis of the test manoeuvres confirmed the accuracy of the predicted aerodynamic data set used for flight clearance. Aircraft handling qualities were very good, particularly so at high incidence where behaviour was described as excellent, much superior to the standard Jaguar with under wing tanks. The air-to-air refuelling task was very easy and straightforward to fly. One pre-flight worry had been the possibility of interaction between the refuelling basket and the aircraft ADD probes. In practice, no difficulties were encountered in this area.

Figure 46 In-flight Refuelling Demonstration

In close formation (and air-to-air tracking) the aircraft could be flown easily and accurately, and spot tracking during a ground attack dive in turbulence was assessed as excellent, twice as good as a standard Jaguar. As with the clean configuration, the aircraft had a tendency to over-respond to turbulence, but never the less, was still rated as easy to fly, even in heavy turbulence. FCS reliability was very good through this phase of flight-testing.

The first flight in the most unstable configuration (strakes plus tanks, a nominal -10% č manoeuvre margin) took place on July 11th 1984, and the trials were successfully completed in only 5 flights. The detailed handling and rapid rolling assessment was performed, together with a more operational assessment comprising air-to-air and air-to-ground tracking, formation flying, air-to-air refuelling with a VC 10 tanker, and aerobatics. Pilot comments were very favourable, with handling characteristics being rated as generally very good, and better than a standard Jaguar by a significant margin. In particular, the operational assessment gave generally excellent results; only in fine tracking was the aircraft less good, with a pitch 'bobble', and somewhat poor initial roll response. Although the aircraft exhibited the same tendency to over-respond in turbulence as happened with the other unstable configurations; however, when compared with the Hunter chase aircraft, the FBW Jaguar response during turbulence penetration was rated as very good. The serviceability of the FCS continued to be very good throughout this phase.

Throughout the straked aircraft flight trials, both project pilots commented on the noticeable performance benefits. Analysis of specific manoeuvres has confirmed this, with significant improvements in lift from the strakes, and worthwhile improvements from the relaxed longitudinal stability.

On completion of the BAe flight assessment, the RAE pilot carried out two separate flight assessments which comprised a total of four flights, two in the clean straked configuration (-4.5% č manoeuvre margin) and 2 in the underwing tank (-10% č manoeuvre margin) configuration. Away from the airfield circuit, RAE pilot comment confirmed the BAe findings. However, in the circuit, and more particularly in turbulence, he found the aircraft somewhat more difficult to fly, commenting that it felt as though there was 'someone else in the cockpit'. In comparison with the BAe pilots, he had not had the same experience of a modern aircraft (Tornado) with its advanced command stability augmentation system (CSAS). This background undoubtedly eased the transition to fully fly-by-wire aircraft.

The appearance of the aircraft at the SBAC Show at Farnborough provided a fitting conclusion to the flying programme. Aircraft performance and serviceability was excellent over the work up and demonstration period, and 22 flights were performed in the clean -4.5% č configuration.

6.8   Pilot Comment 2 – Pete Orme and the Farnborough Air Show 1984

Peter Orme shared the Farnborough Air Show flying with Chris Yeo and he recalled his experience of the 1984 SBAC Farnborough Show as follows.

'This display was shared 50/50 with Chris Yeo with me performing on the first 4 days and Chris covering the last four days. It's always wise to have two pilots trained up for air shows so that if one is incapacitated for some reason, the show can still go on.

We tried to have a common display routine but we couldn't agree on which manoeuvres to perform. From my side, having flown a thousand hours in normal Jaguars, there was one manoeuvre that was particularly difficult to perform consistently in the standard Jaguar and that was a level slow roll. I never once saw a RAF Jaguar perform one at low level. This was because the aircraft had no ailerons and relied on a differential tail plane and wing spoilers for roll control. In addition, the rolling moment due to sideslip was 10 times higher than most other fighter aircraft. This combination meant that precise control of roll rate and flight path during high sideslip manoeuvres such as a slow roll was very difficult and significant altitude excursions were almost inevitable. In squadron service as a ground attack aircraft, this really didn't matter. In contrast, by virtue of the FBW Jaguar's excellent handling qualities stemming from its full authority FCS, a level slow roll was fairly easy to fly. My thinking was that if we were to impress the Jaguar aficionados watching the show, then seeing FBW Jaguar perform a level slow roll at 200 feet above ground would be truly impressive. Thus, this manoeuvre became part of my routine. However, Chris was uncomfortable to committing to such a manoeuvre in the limited time available to work up of our displays and so declined to include it into his routine instead focussing on demonstrating the improved turning performance of FBW Jaguar's unstable configuration and increased wing area compared to a standard Jaguar. Thus we ended up carrying out quite different display routines.

The slow roll manoeuvre went down well. However, I was 'spoken to' by the airworthiness gentlemen after every demo flight (total 19 sequences including practices and air show qualification) for exceeding the negative g limit (some 19 times). This always occurred during the second quarter of the slow roll manoeuvre as the aircraft approached the inverted flight point. Because of the fitting of the inboard leading edge extensions, the aircraft's negative g limit had been cut back from minus 3g to minus 1.8g. This was just enough to do the slow roll at 200 feet above ground level at 400 knots without losing altitude. Just add a bit of turbulence and a bit of fear factor and the result was 19 exceedences of between minus 0.1g and minus 0.2g. My defence was that the g-meter scale wasn't inscribed at minus 1.8g (which was anyway a really silly number to use as a g limit), only at minus 1.5g and minus 2g, and therefore it was a struggle to respect a minus 1.8g limit. So, after each demo flight, the airworthiness men said, 'Bad boy; don't do it again!' I said, 'Sorry, I promise not to do it again.' The flight testers said, 'Hurray, another good data point.' The stress men did a few cross checks using a slightly thicker than normal pencil and said 'It's just OK!' And the show went on. I will be forever impressed by the professionalism, expertise and pragmatism of all those wonderful people who were involved in getting the job done.

Sadly, my last 1984 Farnborough Air Show demonstration flight on Wednesday 5th September was to be my last flight (42nd) in the FBW Jaguar which completed its programme of 96 flights shortly after its return to Warton after the air show.'

7   POST FLYING PROGRAMME

As the main FBW programme came to a close ideas were raised as to the future prospects of further work taking advantage of the aircraft as an existing research asset. During 1983, a proposal was made by Eddy Daley[xxiv] suggesting various topics, and this was discussed with some other ideas at a meeting in December 1983 at RAE Farnborough. Although these proposals were favourably received, there was no real enthusiasm for a further flying programme. This can be attributed in part to the start of the Experimental Aircraft Programme (EAP).

As a result, the only proper use of the Jaguar was as a test bed for research into EMC and test methods. This was a direct follow on of both of the previous EMC tests and the work associated with the Lightning Strike Tests. This work, looking at bulk current injection, was somewhat specialised but vital to ensure that adequate safety margins could be established for future fly-by-wire aircraft. This unglamorous research did not require any flying and so tended to escape attention except in academic circles where a number of papers were given by Ian MacDiarmid.

Following the conclusion of the EMC test programme, the aircraft languished in the open on the south side of Warton aerodrome – according to the accountants it would 'cost' £15,000 a year to store it in the corner of a hangar. It was then used as the test bed for paint treatments turning from bright 'raspberry ripple' to drab green; a very sorry state for such a significant aircraft and for a while it seemed it might be scrapped. Happily, this did not happen and as a result of a tie up between BAe and Loughborough University in January 1991, it was decided to transport the aircraft to Loughborough by road (it was no longer in a flyable condition). Thus for some years it survived (still in drab green) as an object for students to climb over; notionally for use as a ground teaching aid for students from the University's Department of Transport Technology (later the Department of Aeronautical and Automotive Engineering and Transport Studies) for those studying Systems Engineering and Aeronautical Engineering.

In 1996, BAe offered Loughborough EAP as a follow on from the Jaguar and the fly-by-wire aircraft in turn was proposed as a suitable subject for the RAF's museum at Cosford. During 1999, it was returned to Warton for a re-paint into the original 'raspberry ripple' paint scheme (transport provided by RAF Abingdon). It now forms a splendid addition to the museum's collection in the Experimental Flight Shed. Since the EAP has also been presented to Cosford, the two Warton aircraft are now an impressive sight side-by-side in the hangar, though possibly overshadowed by the presence of the much larger TSR.2 (another Warton aircraft) in the centre of the hangar.

Figure 47 The FBW Jaguar at Cosford, seen under the nose of EAP. (D King)

8   CONCLUSION

The aim of the research programme was to be the design, development and demonstration of a safe, practical full time, fly-by-wire flight control system for a combat aircraft. The major constraint on the overall design philosophy was that the overall safety of the research aircraft must not be degraded by the introduction of this system. Thus in the Feasibility Study (reference xi), the primary objective of the programme was stated quite simply as being:

• To generate confidence in the airworthiness of full time FBW

This the programme achieved in full measure.

In summary it achieved:

• First flight of a digital FBW aircraft without any backup (mechanical or analogue) on 20th October 1981

• Software developed and cleared to safety critical standards

• Ground testing to demonstrate full EMC and lightning strike clearance

• Flight demonstration of carefree handling

• Flight demonstration of an aerodynamically unstable aircraft

• Airworthiness procedures identified and confirmed for certification of a full authority digital FCS - now incorporated in DEF STAN 00 970

The FBW Jaguar had its origins in 1974 and first flight in 1981 and so is very much an historical programme using, by later standards, quite primitive computers and software design tools. There was very little experience in the field and the team of mostly young engineers had to undertake the design and invent procedures from scratch. It had the advantage of a very competent manager in Dave Parry, who unlike many of his successors actually understood the job in question and so could ask the right questions – his was in no way management by box ticking. This also meant that his team had the confidence to take responsibility for their actions in a way that is almost unknown today where there is the constant worry of litigation. This means that this type of project would today be almost impossible, certainly within reasonable cost constraints.

It is also notable that of those who worked on this small team, three progressed to board level: Dave Parry, Brian Philipson and Colin Penny[18], whilst several others attained senior management positions.

Thanks to the FBW Jaguar, EAP was developed in a short timescale by people who were now experienced in the design and clearance of FBW aircraft and this in turn led to the success of Eurofighter Typhoon.

---

[18] Colin Penny left the FBW team (and BAe) in 1980 to join General Electric Controls at Johnston City, New York. General Electric Controls was then sold to Martin Marietta, followed by sale to Lockheed and finally to BAE Systems

Figure 48 The Way Forward to EAP and Typhoon: Active Control Technology (Author)

9   APPENDIX 1 – PERSONNEL

Full and part time personnel have been identified as far as possible given the time that has elapsed since the conclusion of the project. Note that not all staff were present throughout the project.

9.1   Feasibility Study (1974 – 1975)

BAC

Leader: BRA Burns (Aerodynamics)

B Gee (Aerodynamics)

IT Darbyshire (Aerodynamics)

K Carr (Aerodynamics)

J Gibson (Aerodynamics)

MJ Walker (Aerodynamics)

JF O'Gara (Flight Test)

RWG Lewis (Hydraulics and actuation)

JP Holding (Hydraulics and actuation)

D Musson (Airworthiness)

D Whittle (Systems)

M Knott (Mechanical Test)

D Corner (Rigs)

BRC Weller (Systems)
(On secondment from BAC Electronics and Space Systems, Bristol)

N Page (Consultant, Electronics and Space Systems, Bristol)

Smiths Industries

KJ Howes

B Williams

Dr JF Meredith

IS Mant

R Griffin

C Richardson

Dowty Boulton Paul

CV Kenmir

DJ Steed

MoD

RW Jones

WE Summerhayes

JLJ Barns

RAE Farnborough (Technical Monitors)

Dr GH Hunt

FR Gill

PWJ Fullam

MJ Corbin

9.2   Main Project (1977 – 1984)

British Aerospace

Early phase, 1977 to 1981

MD Parry (Project and Technical Manager)

JP Holding (Deputy Project Manager), replaced by E Daley.

WA Boardman (Secretary)

Later phases including flight test activities 1981 to 1984

E Daley (Project and Technical Manager)

J Doré (Secretary)

Project Team

BRC Weller (Senior Systems Engineer)

DA Allison (Senior Engineer, Actuation)

IT Darbyshire (Senior Engineer, Aerodynamics)

JR Nelson (Aerodynamics)

AF Young (Systems)

R Dell (Aerodynamics)

D Holmes (Aerodynamics)

C Penny (Systems)

GJ Allen (Systems)

A Agnew (Systems)

DS Nicoll (Systems)

AP Greco (Systems)

P Wood (Systems)

D Norris (Systems)

Aerodynamics

B Gee (Principal Aerodynamicist)

J Gibson (Handling Qualities Specialist)

R Stirling

HT Widger

D Jarvis

M Rigby

A McCuish

A Vause

Rig Team

D Corner

D Baggaley

T Wain

S McKenna

R Brierley

S Burns

RG Calvert

A Bousefield

SP Crompton

D Gasser

Flight Test

TD Smith

P A Doggett

P Culbert

B Philipson

DJ Holmes

CG Norris

Flight Simulation

MR Southworth

P Beckett

N Coleridge Smith

Pilots
CJ Yeo
KP Orme

Procurement
John Hallion

Workshops
A Hibbert (Foreman)
J Taylor
D Edmundson
F Hoyle
A Blackstock
J Oddie

Inspection
B Page (Mech Inspection)
P Swindells (Elect Inspection)

Other Departments
E Kendal (Reliability)
AT Drysdale (Reliability)
W Bradshaw (Airworthiness)
D Beck (Maths Services)
S Brown (Maths Services)
IP MacDiarmid (EMC and Lightning)
B Entwistle (Electronics)
A Welch (Electronics)
J Westmoreland (Electronics)
B Gleaves (Electronics)
H Bell (P&D Test)
R Lakin (P&D Test)

RAE Farnborough (Technical Monitors)
Dr GH Hunt
FR Gill
M Watts
MJ Corbin

Dowty Boulton Paul
Actuator Design
CV Kenmir (Chief Engineer)
DJ Steed (Project leader and performance analysis)
AD Mountney (Chief Designer)
G Attfield (Design)
W Prosser (Design)
D Nicholls (Design)
J Grainger (Chief Electrical Design)
D Lockley (Electrical Installation)
D Hammond (Chief Stressman)
K Smith (Stress)
N Webb (Weights)
J Roper (Analysis)
I Mansfield (Analysis)
P Gibons (Analysis)
Note: 'Analysis' covers performance, simulation, specifications, test documentation and reliability

Test Rigs and Testing

G Newman (Mechanical Rig Design)

A Smart (Chief Electronics Engineer)

T Clayton (Electronics Design)

T Benton (Electrical and Electronics)

Note: T Benton did the design and manufacture of the then novel matched LVDTs.

T Herrington (Chief Development Engineer)

G Garnett (Development and Environmental Test)

Manufacture

R Fellows (Experimental Machine Shop Supervisor)

R Wells (Production Manufacturing Support)

J Morton (Production Manufacturing Support)

R Briggs (Production Manufacturing Support)

Cost Control

V Doughty Company Cost Accounting)

G Ward (Engineering Cost Control)

Marconi-Elliott (MAv) (later GEC Avionics)

Directors (throughout)

J Pateman (Managing Director)

W Alexander

P Hearne

R Howard (Technical Director)

Proposal Phase

D Jackson (Divisional Manager)

R George (Proposal Manager)

H Pearce (Project Manager)

K Snelling (Engineering Manager)

R B Smith (Hardware and Systems Engineering)

K Barton (Hardware and Systems Engineering)

K Rosenberg (Software and Systems Engineering)

T Egan (Software)

I Newton (Hardware and Systems Engineering)

J Corney (Systems Engineering)

Support from Flight Aviation Research Lab under Dick Collinson

Project Phase

There were various changes to staff, particularly as the design evolved and problems with specific items had to be resolved.

J Spinks (Divisional Manager)

G Belcher (Technical Manager)

K Snelling (Engineering Manager)

H Pearce (Project Manager), replaced by

R E Marshall (Project Manager)

EA Fosbeary (Project Controller)

R B Smith (technical support as necessary and safety analysis)

M Tomsett (Quality Assurance Manager) plus his team

I Newton (provided technical support in early part of programme)

K Barton (Hardware Engineering and EMC)

N Chatfield (Hardware Engineering – Digital)

T Egan (Software Engineering), replaced by

M Gibson (Software Engineering)

F King (Software Engineering, early phases)

M Watts (Software Engineering, later phases)

N White (Hardware Engineering, later phases)

K Rosenberg (Systems Engineering)

R Heaps (Hardware Engineering, later Systems Engineering and 'Lab Ram')

J K Jones (Hardware Engineering)

C Berry (Hardware Engineering)

A Thornton (Hardware Engineering, later phases)

S Morgan (Hardware Engineering, later phases)

L Jarvis (Hardware Engineering)

J Gilson (Environmental Test Support)

H Foan (Environmental Test Support)

C Munro (Environmental Test Support)

C Elmore (Test Equipment)

G Paternoster (Model Shop Superintendent) and his team

A Scoones (On-site team at Warton)

RS Lewis (On-site team at Warton)

REFERENCES

[i] A. Seabridge and L. Skorczewski, 'The Experimental Aircraft Programme, Britain's Last Manned Aircraft Demonstrator', BAE Systems plc, 2016.

[ii] Wilber Wright, 'Some Aeronautical Experiments', address to the Western Society of Engineers, September 1901.

[iii] BAC & Aérospatiale, 'Concorde Engineering Notes Section 9, Flying Controls and Flight Control System', C472/9, 1973.

[iv] W. Haeussermann, 'Developments in the Field of Automatic Guidance and Control of Rockets', J. Guidance and Control, May-June 1981.

[v] B.R.A. Burns, 'Control-Configured Combat Aircraft', 1978

[vi] Wolfgang J. Kubbat, Head Flugführung (Guidance and Control), Messerschmitt-Bölkow-Blohm GmbH, D-8 München 80, Germany, 'A Quadruredundant [sic] Digital, Flight Control System for CCV Application'.

[vii] B.R.A. Burns, 'Research Proposal 'Design Study of the Installation of an Integrated Fly-by-wire Flight Control System in a Jaguar in co-operation with Smith's Industries Ltd.', Ae/R/121, July 1974.

[viii] 'Advanced Control Systems for Manned Aircraft', Hawker Siddeley Aviation Ltd., YPO 819, March 1974.

[ix] R. Melling, 'Advanced Control Systems for Manned Aircraft, Draft Proposals for Flight Testing', Hawker Siddeley Aviation Ltd., YPO 855, June 1974.

[x] J.F Meredith, 'Echo and Iago Effects', Smiths ACS/DFS/6, February 1975.

[xi] B.R.A. Burns, 'Design Study of the Installation of an Integrated Fly-by-Wire Control System in a Jaguar in Conjunction with Smith's Industries Limited and Dowty Boulton Paul Limited', JAG/FBW/25, September 1975.

[xii] G.C. Howell, 'Flight Experience of a Rate Demand Control using Electric Signalling in the Avro 707C Aircraft', AGARD Report 536, May 1966.

[xiii] B. Williams, 'Configurations for a Full-Time Fly-by-wire System Resulting from Discussions with Hydraulic Actuator Manufactures', Smiths RID-1449, October 1974.

[xiv] Space Navigation, Guidance and Control, Miller editor, AGARD 105.

[xv] C.R. Jarvis, 'A Digital Fly-By-Wire Technology Program Using an F-8C Test Aircraft,' AIAA 74-28, 12th Aerospace Sciences Meeting, Washington, D.C., Jan. 30–Feb.1, 1974.

[xvi] B.R.C. Weller, 'Jaguar FBW Electrical Power Supplies', 8539/BRCW/MM/9, February 1975.

[xvii] R.B. Smith, Jaguar Fly-by-Wire Integrated Flight Control System Integrity Appraisal, MAv JTR 093, Sept 1981

[xviii] AO Ward and BRC Weller, 'Testing Software', Quality Assurance of Software, Defence Quality Assurance Board Executive, London, 13 March 1980.

[xix] H.T. Widger, 'Jaguar FBW Flight Control System and Autopilot Control Law Requirements', JAG/FBW/156, final issue 10, January 1984.

[xx] A.W. Hanson (Culham Lab), letter to H.B. Johnston (RAE Farnborough) on whole aircraft lightning strike tests, E11A-1, 29 October 1979.

[xxi] P.A. Doggett, meeting minutes, 'FBW Jaguar Proposed Simulated Lightning Strike Tests', JAG/20.7/PAD/MV/09D81, 9 December 1981.

[xxii] P.A. Doggett, 'FBW Jaguar : Whole Aircraft Simulated Lightning Strike Tests : Final Report', JAG/FBW/346, August 1982.

[xxiii] T.D. Smith, 'Final Report on the Jaguar FBW Programme on Research in Active Control Technology', JAG/FBW/492, December 1984.

[xxiv] E. Daley, 'Jaguar FBW - Future Programme ', 853/ED/JMD/208/8.28, July 1983.

About the Author

Brian Weller graduated from the University of Surrey in 1972 with a degree in Electronic and Electrical Engineering. Interest in aircraft engineering was stimulated by spending a year at the Royal Aircraft Establishment Farnborough as part of the course and by lectures from Dr Barnes Wallis and Sir George Edwards, the latter being head of BAC at that time. This led to him joining what was then the British Aircraft Corporation at Bristol in 1972 where he worked on detailed electronic design for the Concorde Air Intake Control System. His next major project was at Warton, system design and safety analysis for the fly-by-wire Jaguar aircraft. Following first flight of the Jaguar in 1981, he moved onto the precursors of Typhoon, initially P110 and then through ACA (the Agile Combat Aircraft, joint with Italy and Germany) to EAP (the Experimental Aircraft Project), which achieved its first flight in 1986.

During the 1980s, much time (over four years) was spent in Munich, Germany, on the design and specification of the Flight Control System for Typhoon. On his return to the UK in 1989, he rejoined the Research Department, and took over the running of the Integrated Flight and Propulsion Control System (IFPCS) project as Chief Engineer in 1993. During the 1990s, assistance was also given to Hindustan Aeronautics on a consultancy basis for the Indian Light Combat Aircraft with several trips out to Bangalore.

On the conclusion of IFPCS in 2000, he acted as an internal consultant (Technologist) on flight control matters. This included working with Dassault on a joint technology demonstration programme, additional trips to India and on the design of the Hawk Mk 128 autopilot. Final involvement at Warton was on the initial design of the Stability Augmentation System for the Nimrod MRA4.

He retired from BAE Systems at the end of 2005.

Warton's Heritage Department

The Heritage Department at Warton, previously known as the BAE Systems North West Heritage Group, was established in June 1995 by a group of volunteers following an appeal by the Company to help support its heritage policy. The Department covers the heritage of the Company in Lancashire, namely the sites at Warton, Samlesbury and formerly Preston.

The Department now has over 40 active volunteers whose range of activities include the establishment and management of document, photographic and film archives. The material held by the Department is used to promote the proud heritage of the Company at various displays and exhibitions as well as answering a constant stream of enquiries from within and outside the Company and producing heritage publications such as this one on the history of the FBW Jaguar.

The Department are always keen to hear from past and present employees who may have material or personal stories that would be of interest.

Finally, do you have a story to tell that you feel would be a good subject for a future heritage publication? If so, please contact us and we will be pleased to discuss your ideas further.

Ian Lawrenson
Heritage Manager - Warton
BAE Systems Heritage Department (W298)
Warton Aerodrome
Nr Preston
Lancashire
PR4 1AX
Tel: 07793 420193
Email: ian.lawrenson@baesystems.com

Heritage Department publications:

- The English Electric P.1 Supersonic Fighter Concept
  (Keith Emslie)

- The Wind Tunnel Department at Warton Aerodrome
  (Keith Emslie)

- Test Flying in Lancashire from Samlesbury and Warton Aerodromes:
  Volume 1: WW1 to the 1960s
  (James H. Longworth)

- Test Flying in Lancashire from Samlesbury and Warton Aerodromes:
  Volume 2: From the 1960s into the 1980s
  (James H. Longworth)

- Test Flying in Lancashire from Samlesbury and Warton Aerodromes:
  Volume 3: From the 1980s into the New Millennium
  (James H. Longworth)

- Dick, Kerr & Co. Limited, Engineers and Contractors:
  London, Kilmarnock and Preston. A History of the Company 1853 - 1919
  (John Shorrock)

- The Experimental Aircraft Programme, Britain's Last Manned Aircraft Demonstrator
  (Allan Seabridge and Leon Skorczewski)